NORTH SHORE FISH

BY ISRAEL HOROVITZ

★

★

DRAMATISTS
PLAY SERVICE
INC.

NORTH SHORE FISH
Copyright © 1989, Israel Horovitz

All Rights Reserved

CAUTION: Professionals and amateurs are hereby warned that performance of NORTH SHORE FISH is subject to payment of a royalty. It is fully protected under the copyright laws of the United States of America, and of all countries covered by the International Copyright Union (including the Dominion of Canada and the rest of the British Commonwealth), and of all countries covered by the Pan-American Copyright Convention, the Universal Copyright Convention, the Berne Convention, and of all countries with which the United States has reciprocal copyright relations. All rights, including without limitation professional/amateur stage rights, motion picture, recitation, lecturing, public reading, radio broadcasting, television, video or sound recording, all other forms of mechanical, electronic and digital reproduction, transmission and distribution, such as CD, DVD, the Internet, private and file-sharing networks, information storage and retrieval systems, photocopying, and the rights of translation into foreign languages are strictly reserved. Particular emphasis is placed upon the matter of readings, permission for which must be secured from the Author's agent in writing.

The English language stock and amateur stage performance rights in the United States, its territories, possessions and Canada for NORTH SHORE FISH are controlled exclusively by DRAMATISTS PLAY SERVICE, INC., 440 Park Avenue South, New York, NY 10016. No professional or nonprofessional performance of the Play may be given without obtaining in advance the written permission of DRAMATISTS PLAY SERVICE, INC., and paying the requisite fee.

Inquiries concerning all other rights should be addressed to Washington Square Arts, 310 Bowery, 2nd Floor, New York, NY 10012. Attn: Bruce Miller.

SPECIAL NOTE

Anyone receiving permission to produce NORTH SHORE FISH is required to give credit to the Author as sole and exclusive Author of the Play on the title page of all programs distributed in connection with performances of the Play and in all instances in which the title of the Play appears for purposes of advertising, publicizing or otherwise exploiting the Play and/or a production thereof. The name of the Author must appear on a separate line, in which no other name appears, immediately beneath the title and in size of type equal to 50% of the size of the largest, most prominent letter used for the title of the Play. No person, firm or entity may receive credit larger or more prominent than that accorded the Author.

SPECIAL NOTE ON SONGS AND RECORDINGS

For performances of copyrighted songs, arrangements or recordings mentioned in this Play, the permission of the copyright owner(s) must be obtained. Other songs, arrangements or recordings may be substituted provided permission from the copyright owner(s) of such songs, arrangements or recordings is obtained; or songs, arrangements or recordings in the public domain may be substituted.

"North Shore Fish" is dedicated
to the memory of Gail Randazza.

PREFACE

When I was a 10-year-old, growing up in Wakefield, Massachusetts, my sister and I were taken to Gloucester by our parents on our family's "special days".

As a 25-year-old, I began living in New York City, zealously "being a New York Playwright", only wandering off my newfound island home for playwrights conferences and regional theatre productions, here and there. (I carefully avoided my native Massachusetts as if it were Philadelphia.)

Some years later, threatened by the prospect of still another summer in the city, I looked about for a place to rent as a vacation-house, and thought, "Why not put my summers down where special days are spent: Gloucester?"

Soon after my toes re-touched Gloucester sand and sea, I thought "Why not put a _life_ down where special days are spent?" I bought a tiny Victorian house, high on a hill, overlooking Gloucester harbor to one side and Good Harbor Beach to the other. It was to have been a weekend house. First visit, I stayed put for 16 consecutive months without returning to NYC for more than a day. My wife and I have made that very house "home base" for the past decade. Our 3-year-old twins were born there. They are Gloucester kids.

About Heroism in Gloucester, Massachusetts. Although Hopper and Sloane and Homer lived and painted in Gloucester, and T.S. Eliot and Charles Olson lived and wrote in Gloucester, Gloucester's heroes never were and never will be painters or writers. Gloucester's heroes are fishermen and carpenters. Gloucester is proud to be a working-class town.

Ten years ago, I founded a small theatre in Gloucester, thinking "if I'm to put my life down here, I'll have to have a place to work." And ten years later, The Gloucester Stage Company is thriving. We are a tiny potato, but a brilliant [says I] tiny potato. The GSC is a 150-seat Equity theatre, housed in a huge old warehouse overlooking the inner harbor. We produce between 8 and 10 plays a year, many of them new American and British plays. I have "tried out" all of my new plays during the past decade in Gloucester at the GSC. And for the past several years, I have been hard at work writing a cycle of plays that are actually set in Gloucester. These Gloucester-based plays have as their central ambition the showing of life as we live(d) it on our little dot on the planet Earth. No more, no less.

My father was a truck-driver who went to law school, nights, and at the age of 50 made a lawyer of himself. During my childhood, I often rode with father in his truck, hauling bales of newspaper to the paper mills in Fitchburg and Lawrence. Not surprisingly, I am as comfortable with working-class people as I am with playwrights and poets. And not surprisingly, my recent plays have dealt with blue-collar life and changing times in the work-place, as lived in our small, coastal city in Massachusetts.

The first of my Gloucester-based plays to surface in NYC was the play published herein, "North Shore Fish", which showed at the WPA Theatre, 2 seasons ago, and now threatens a Broadway transfer. (Although "North Shore Fish" gathered about the most favorable reviews any play of mine has ever gathered from the NYC drama critics—plus nominations for both the Pulitzer Prize and for The New York Drama Desk Award—the play still awaits a commercial, open-ended production in NYC. The cast is large and the producers are waiting for what they call "viable stars". No comment.) Last season, a Gloucester-based comedy, "Year Of The Duck", made its way into the new season at the Hudson Guild Theatre. And now, this current season in NYC features a GSC/Working Theatre collaborative production of my Gloucester-based

"Henry Lumper", off-Broadway, at The Actors Outlet Theatre. "Henry Lumper" is the "brother play" to "North Shore Fish". If "North Shore Fish" is the story of "The Girls", "Henry Lumper" is clearly, the story of "The Boys". (A Lumper is a stevedore. The waterfront-workers' union is, by the way, comprised of both groups: Lumpers and "girls" from the fish-processing plants. Union leadership has always been male-dominated.)

By way of background for this specific play, Gloucester was for some 300 years, first and foremost, a working-class city, an international seaport. Livings were made "on the water", hunting fish or lobster, or "workin' the wharfs", cutting and packing fish in the processing plants.

During the past decade, Gloucester gained national attention for three local commodities: "Moonies", waterfront real estate and hard drugs. The hottest issue by far was what the newspapers called "The Moonie Issue". Boston's beloved Richard Cardinal Cushing somehow approved (if not engineered) the sale of a massive piece of Gloucester property to Rev. Moon, leader of the Unification Church, a world-wide religious organization best known for its mass weddings, and for the sale of more tinned tuna than any other fish-hunter on the planet Earth. Gloucester people were at once certain their innocent children would be drugged and kidnapped by the "Moonies". On the side of Reality, the "Moonie" fishing fleet actually did undercut local fish prices, and by a lot. Racism exploded. T-shirts appeared on the chests of otherwise sane Gloucester family folks headlining such legends as "Save Gloucester—Shoot a Moonie!"

But Time does have its way. No Gloucester children were drugged or kidnapped. Fish prices came into (relative) balance. T-shirts and picket-lines faded and the other two Gloucester commodities worthy of nationwide media attention stepped forward in Gloucester people's hearts and minds. According to the Boston Globe, in 1986, Gloucester real estate prices were reckoned to be the "most inflated in the nation". And according to the Boston Globe, in 1987, Gloucester's drug problem, was "the worst in the nation".

In the simplest possible terms, local real estate prices and local wages became absurdly disproportionate. A local person could sell his house, instantly, for an amount equal to ten years' wages. No local young couple could possibly afford to buy a 1st-time home. A fisherman could earn more money carrying a cigar box filled with cocaine than he could earn in a month of fishing.

And any local business that happened to be housed on the waterfront could be sold to condo developers for ten times its actual worth. Business sold. The fishing industry was damaged beyond repair. Entire categories of work became virtually obsolete. In short, women whose mothers and grandmothers and great-grandmothers and great-great-grandmothers had stood shoulder-to-shoulder "on the line", processing and packing, suddenly found processing plants were closed. There was no call for the only sort of work they were trained to do.

What happens to people's dignity when their work is no longer useful or available?

In frustration, a shocking number of Gloucester people sold their homes, sold out. And an even more shocking number of Gloucester's young people began selling drugs ... and using drugs.

When The Gloucester Stage Company first workshopped "Henry Lumper" in Gloucester, a few years ago, one of the stage mums, a young woman named Gail Randazza, filled my head — and my play — with vivid detail of Gloucester's drug problem. She confessed to me that there was "a junkie in the family", and therefore she "really knew the problem intimately." I daresay all too intimately. A few months after we first met, Gail died from a heroin overdose. She was a single parent, a mother of three. Gail had been a cutter and packer in a local fish-packing plant, as had been her mother and her grandmother and great-grandmother for decades before her. During the final weeks of her former employer's processing plant, she snuck me into the work-rooms several times so that I could do some first-hand research for the imagined fish-processing plant of my play "North Shore Fish". Gail told me "both my plant and my plans closed down ... same day".

Gail became the model for Florence, the lead character in "North Shore Fish". (I have subsequently dedicated the play to her, as well.) It seems to me that all too often the most and the best we playwrights can do when life serves up unthinkably high drama is to write it down.

Upon learning of Gail's death, I wrote an essay for the local paper that was featured in the Editor's "Hold" bin for several weeks and then printed as a "Letter To The Editor". Somehow, the Boston Globe picked up this obscure little news piece and managed to track me down in NYC. I was interviewed for several hours over the next few weeks' time, and, to my amazement, the Globe soon ran a month-long, in depth front-page series on the drug traffic in historic, picturesque Gloucester, Massachusetts.

Gloucester began to face its problem.

"North Shore Fish" doesn't deal with the specific issues of "The Moonies" or Gloucester's dreaded drug-traffic. ("Henry Lumper" hits both issues head-on.) "North Shore Fish" focusses instead on the role of women in Gloucester's working-class society, and, of course, on the issue of work-categories becoming virtually obsolete. "North Shore Fish" is, to my thinking, a play about love and dignity in the work-place.

And now the play is being printed and offered for production all over the world.

There is always concern that a play like "North Shore Fish" might be "too Gloucester" to be effective and interesting to a larger world. I have long believed that all knowledge flows through the trunk of the tree. This is to say if we know one thing completely — totally — we know all things. Thus, a great brain surgeon also knows great carpentry, by simply applying the same logic he applies to brain surgery. Insofar as my Gloucester-based plays are concerned, I believe that if I am truly successful in my dramatising of life as it is really lived — if the Gloucester detail is expertly observed — then the play will have meaning and will touch people throughout the world.

The fact that "North Shore Fish" was well received by New Yorkers bodes very well indeed for the play's future outside Gloucester. (To my delight, there is already a completed French translation and a large commercial production planned for Paris.)

I cannot imagine anything more gratifying — more exciting to me, really — than my tossing of a rock into the sea at Gloucester, and watching the ripples fan out and out and out — to a world beyond.

I am a lucky fellow.

> Israel Horovitz
> New York City — Gloucester, Mass.,
> February, 1989.

NORTH SHORE FISH was given its World Premiere on August 24, 1986, at the Gloucester Stage Company (Israel Horovitz, Artistic Director/Producer; Grey Cattell Johnson, Associate Artistic Director). It was directed by Grey Cattell Johnson, with sets by David Condino, costumes by Jeanine Phaneuf Burgess, and lighting by B. N. Productions. The cast, in order of appearance, was as follows:

ALFRED (PORKER) MARTINO............ Mark Rogers
FLORENCE RIZZO.................. Geraldine Librandi
ARLYNE FLYNN .... Mary Klug
RUTHIE................................ Judith McIntrye
SALVATORE (SALLY) MORELLA.... Theodore Reinstein
JOSEPHINE EVANGELISTA.............. Michelle Faith
MAUREEN VEGA .... Karen Crawford
MARLENA............................. Teade Gormley
CATHERINE SHIMMA..................... Tara Dolan

It then went on to a New York production at the WPA Theatre (Kyle Renick, Artistic Director; Wendy Bustard, Managing Director), opening on January 12, 1987. Directed by Stephen Zuckerman, it had sets by Edward T. Gianfrancesco, lights by Craig Evans, costumes by Mimi Maxmen, sound by Aural Fixation, the Production Stage Manager was David Lawrence Folender, and the cast was as follows:

ALFRED (PORKER) MARTINO .... John Pankow
FLORENCE RIZZO .... Christine Estabrook
ARLYNE FLYNN .... Mary Klug
RUTHIE .... Cordelia Richards
SALVATORE (SALLY) MORELLA..... Thomas G. Waites
JOSEPHINE EVANGELISTA .... Michelle M. Faith
MAUREEN VEGA .... Elizabeth Kemp
MARLENA......................... Laura San Giacomo
CATHERINE SHIMMA.................. Wendie Malick

THE PEOPLE OF THE PLAY

ALFRED "PORKER" MARTINO, 30's, small, sadly comic.

FLORENCE RIZZO, 30's, once a high-school bombshell.

ARLYNE FLYNN, late 50's, thin, nervous; Ruthie's mother.

RUTHIE FLYNN, 30's, adorable; enormously pregnant.

SALVATORE "SALLY" MORELLA, early 30's; lean, handsome.

JOSIE EVANGELISTA, 30's, strikingly plump.

MAUREEN VEGA, 30's, tall, thin, bespectacled.

MARLENA VEGA, 30's, Maureen's cousin; quite beautiful: the new girl.

CATHERINE SHIMMA, 30's, slightly up-market look.

THE PLACE OF THE PLAY

Assembly-line and main plant, North Shore Fish, a frozen fish processing company in Gloucester, Massachusetts.

THE TIME OF THE PLAY

A work-day in Summer, the Present.

THE ACCENT OF THE PLAY

Massachusetts North Shore accent, as in "Park Your Car in Harvard Yard".

A NOTE ON THE SET

The set should be primarily stage scenery, but combined with components of actual assembly-line machinery.

Generally speaking, the machinery that would be correctly used for "North Shore Fish" would be outmoded, obsolete. The feel of the plant should be old and out of date.

Although only one assembly-line is functional, there might be another assembly-line in view.

There is a large glass-windowed office overhead, probably centre-stage, housing the Inspector's Kitchen. This office is kitted-out with desk, typewriter, scale, stove. The office should have a solid door, so that a full-blown argument in the office, upstairs, would only present an angry murmur of sound to the workers, downstairs, on the "line". Anyone in the office, however, is totally visible to plant workers and audience alike. The overall effect of the office is that of a 2nd stage [or a gigantic movie screen or television monitor inhabited by live actors, acting] suspended over the primary stage.

North Shore Fish Processing Co., Inc. has seen better days, in years past. This fact should be made clear by the shabbiness of the plant, and by its accumulated clutter.

Each station of the assembly-line is personalized with a small open box upon which the name of the worker has been magic-markered. Thus, there are boxes marked "Flo", "Ruthie". "Arlyne", "Josie",

"Trish", "Zoe", "Carmella", "Slugger" and "Hazel".

Trash containers are clean corrugated-cardboard cartons, tall, lined with clear plastic bags that are collared around the topmost edge of the cartons, awaiting filling and closure. There is a carton at every functional station of the entire "line" and there is a stack of stock cartons forming a huge mass on the upstage wall.

Pipes, ducts chains, cables and other "high-tech" trappings are in evidence everywhere.

The assembly-lines have two major conveyor systems: one to bring raw product to the workers; the second to bring finished product to the wrapping table.

A NOTE ON THE COSTUMING

White or pastel dresses and aprons, rubber or disposable plastic gloves, hairnets and netted visor "caps", for the women. Porker wears short-sleeved chino shirt, matching chino pants, high rubber gloves, white apron, rubber boots, Red Sox cap. Sally wears tight-fitting blue gabardine slacks, black loafers, striped shirt and tie, long white coat. He sometimes wears hard-hat. Catherine wears skirt, blouse, sweater, white coat over all.

NORTH SHORE FISH

ACT ONE

Lights up on line of machinery, interior of fish-processing plant. 1940's assembly-line fills stage. Aluminum vats, white-rubber conveyor belt, cement floor, vast space all around. A glass-windowed office overlooks the "line" from above, centre-stage.

Porker Martino, early 30's, mops floor. As he mops, he sings "Strangers In The Night"*, taking liberties with song's lyrics. He wears chino pants and shirt; Red Sox cap.

PORKER.
Strangers in the night ...
Exchanging glances ...
Strangers in the night ...
Taking our chances ...
We made out all right ...
Because of lovvvve ...
How would we have guessed? ...Dum duh dah
Dum dahh *(Forgets lyrics completely.)* ...
I forget the rest ... *(Improvises.)*
Love was just a glance away ...
A warm romantic chance away ... *(Heading toward a big finish.)*
We made out all right ...
Taking our chances ...

*"STRANGERS IN THE NIGHT"
Words by CHARLES SINGLETON & EDDIE SNYDER
Music by BERT KAEMPFERT
© Copyright 1966 by CHAMPION MUSIC CORPORATION. Rights administered by MCA MUSIC PUBLISHING, A Division of MCA INC., New York, NY 10019.
USED BY PERMISSION   ALL RIGHTS RESERVED

Lovers at first sight ...
Take off your pants-es ...
She wasn't too bright ...
But, we were strangers in the *nighhhhhtttttt!**

(Florence enters, wearing shorts, bright blouse, sunglasses, carrying two largish pocketbooks, cigarette in her lips. She rubs her hands together, warming them. She listens to Porker's big finish before commenting. Her comment startles him.)

FLORENCE. Jesus, Porker, that you *singin'?* I thought they were stranglin' fuckin' *dolphins* in here! I never would'a guessed you were stranglin' fuckin' "Strangers In The Night".

PORKER. You sound like a *toilet*, you know that?

FLORENCE. You *are* a toilet! What a sketch, Porker! Moppin' and singin' like whatisname ... Andy Williams ... *(Pulls her blouse over her head. She wears a lacy bra.)* Turn your head around! I'm changin'!

PORKER. *(Looks away.)* Frank Sinatra, dumbbell ...

FLORENCE. How old's he? Eighty?

PORKER. Yuh, right, eighty, you got it ... *(Florence goes to closet and removes freshly ironed pastel green smock, which she pulls over her head. She puts her blouse in closet.)*

FLORENCE. I'm takin' my pants off ...

PORKER. What am I? S'pose'ta'get *excited?*

FLORENCE. Just turn your head around! You're s'pose'ta be moppin', that's all, so *mop!*

PORKER. Hard ta' get anything much worked up around your pants comin' off, I can tell you that! It's kinda' like gettin' excited about a wave hittin' Good Harbor Beach. *(Florence folds her shorts into the closet with her blouse neatly. Porker continues.)* First couple'a waves, you yell "Oh, wow, lookit! A wave!" But, after fifty or sixty thousand waves, it's kinda' hard ta' get anything much worked up in the excitement department, if you follow my message ...

FLORENCE. What the Christ are you talkin' about, Porker?

PORKER. Your *pants*, Florence! After you take your pants on and

---

*Used by special permission. See copyright page.

off fifty or sixty thousand times, it don't make much of no impression on anybody ...
FLORENCE. Oh, right, I get you, Porker. It's a *jokkke* ... about me takin' my pants off a lot counta' I'm in and out of bed ...
PORKER. *(Adds an "s".)* zs*ssszzz* ...
FLORENCE. Bed*ssszzz* ... Well, I guess you must be jealous, bein' left out and all, counta you got no dick ...
PORKER. I do okay ...
FLORENCE. Is that a fact?
PORKER. What's a *dolphin*, anyhow? Like in the circus kind'a thing?
FLORENCE. Dolphins are grey mammals. Dolphins are smart. They got brains. They talk to each other. They got their own language. They *frolic!*
PORKER. I frolic ...
FLORENCE. Bullllshhhittt you frolic, Porker. You're a hundred per cent glum all the time and you know it! You are next ta' pathetic! What's with the air-conditioning? It's freezing in here.
PORKER. I already turned it down ...
FLORENCE. What's Markie planning? Ta' freeze the help and cut us up inta' *fillettes?*
PORKER. I already turned it down! *(Arlyne enters with Ruthie, who is enormously pregnant. Both women are smoking. both carry coffee thermoses under their arms, drink from plastic coffee cups as they enter. They walk directly to their lockers.)*
FLORENCE. *(Sudden sweetness; to Arlyne.)* Mornin', Arlyne. How's the hip?
ARLYNE. Rough, still, thanks, Floey. How's yo'r Mum?
FLORENCE. Doin' better, thanks ...
ARLYNE. Mornin', Porker. Freezin' in here ...
PORKER. I already turned it down ...
FLORENCE. He already turned it down. Mornin', Ruthie.
PORKER. Mornin', Ruthie ...
RUTHIE. Mornin', Floey ... Mornin', Porker ...
FLORENCE. No change, huh?
RUTHIE. Nothin'. I'm ten months, as of this mornin'. Dr.

Benoit's definitely got my due date wrong. I'm thinkin' of changin' doctors, to tell you the truth ... *(Ruthie stops talking, suddenly, as Sally Morella enters. He is thin, handsome, thirty. He wears a white shirt, tie, long white coat, open; hard-hat. Without noticing or acknowledging anyone, he runs up the staircase into kitchen in glass-windowed office about the "line". He tidies up the place, fussing about, nervously readying kitchen for new Inspector, he Windexes the kitchen window. He plumps pillow on desk-chair. He arranges pens on desk.)* What's with Sal?

PORKER. New government inspector starts today ...

RUTHIE. Oh, yuh, right. So, how're the kids, Flo?

FLORENCE. Ungrateful, late for school, usual stuff ... Bradley said he had a headache, so, I said "You're seven, Bradley, you can't have a headache 'til you're ten ..." He says "Who says?" and I says "It's a fact, everybody knows it, boys don't get headaches 'til then and girls don't get 'em til twelve, 'cause they're smarter ..." Then, Emily screams "You hear that, Breadloaf? Girls are smarter!" And Bradley throws his goddam egg at her!

ARLYNE. Nooo!

FLORENCE. Yesss!

ARLYNE. Little boys can be very mean to little girls.

PORKER. Raw?

FLORENCE. What's this?

PORKER. The egg: raw?

FLORENCE. Scrambled, shitforbrains! What? You think I feed my kids raw eggs?

ARLYNE. This mornin'?

FLORENCE. Less than an hour ago ...

RUTHIE. What'd Emily do? She muckle him, or what?

FLORENCE. No, not much. Bradley's got her scared. I think he hits on her when I'm not home yet ... *(Pauses.)* She cried ... *(There is a pause.)* Either of you see the dolphins on TV, last night ...?

RUTHIE. With the guy speakin' French or something?

FLORENCE. Jock-something, yuh. You see it?

RUTHIE. I switched over. I couldn't stand the foreign words ...

FLORENCE. There was a simultaneous translation ... in English ... a guy was translating over the French ... at the same time.
RUTHIE. Yuh, but I didn't like it ... And Earl gets really pissed off when they talk foreign on the TV.
FLORENCE. The dolphins were so wicked smart ...
ARLYNE. I remember, years back, there was a TV show every week. What was it called?
RUTHIE. I don't know why they don't just put American shows on the TV? I don't know who they think they're tryin' ta' please by puttin' all this French crap on. I'll bet we don't have more'n two Frenchman livin' on Cape Ann, period ...
ARLYNE. Uncle Ben?
RUTHIE. That's rice, Ma ...
ARLYNE. Something like that ... There was a show with a "Ben" ...
PORKER. "Gentle Ben" ...
ARLYNE. That's it! That was great!
PORKER. *(To Florence, confidentially.)* Stupid fuckin' show ...
FLORENCE. *(Sees that Arlyne is embarrassed.)* Will you watch your tongue, cesspool?
PORKER. If that ain't the teapot callin' the fryin' pan black ... *(The three women giggle. Porker is perplexed.)* What's funny? What's so goddam funny? *(Sally pokes head out of upstairs office. He calls down to the women.)*
SALLY. Mornin', girls ...
ARLYNE & RUTHIE. Mornin' Sally ... Hey, Sal ...
SALLY. Hey, Florence, you got a minute?
FLORENCE. In front of everybody? *(Giggles from all.)*
SALLY. Very comical.
PORKER. Big day, huh, Sally? You ready for this, or what?
SALLY. What's this?
PORKER. You kiddin' me?
SALLY. That? No big deal there ta' *me!*
PORKER. You seen her yet?
SALLY. Makes no nevermind to me, whatsoever! *(To Florence.)* Can I just see you, please? *(Sal exits into Inspector's Office, again,*

closing door behind him. Florence laughs, goes up the stairs to Sally. She enters Office, closes door behind her. NOTE: Sally and Florence are now visible to audience through Office window. Maureen and Marlena enter, all in late 30's. Maureen and Marlena cross and exit off-stage, to changing room, smiling to Porker as they go.)

MAUREEN. Mornin', Porker ... How's the weekend?

PORKER. Not bad, not bad. Yourself?

MAUREEN. Good. It's freezing in here.

PORKER. I turned it down already. *(Sees Marlena.)* This her?

MAUREEN. Yup.

PORKER. How's it goin'?

MARLENA. How's yourself?

MAUREEN. Where's Floey? She sick again? *(Arlyne and Ruthie point straight above their heads, as if pointing to Heaven.)*

PORKER. Company business. *(Maureen looks up at window.* NOTE: *We now see Florence and Sal are in a passionate embrace.)*

MARLENA. Wow! Who's that?

MAUREEN. I'll tell ya' later. Come on ... *(Maureen and Marlena exit. Josie enters. She is strikingly plump.)*

ARLYNE. Morning, Josephine ...

RUTHIE. Morning, Josie ... How goes it?

JOSIE. Morning, Arlyne. Morning, Ruthie. It's cold in here ... Where's Florence? Sick again? *(Everybody points straight up. Josie looks up and shakes her head in mock disgust.)* They were doin' that when I left here, yesterday. They been there all *night? (Josie crosses to her locker, touching Porker's shoulder as she passes him.)* Mornin', Porker ...

PORKER. Yo, Josie, what's up? ... I turned the air-conditioner down already. New shirt, huh, Jose*? * *(Rhymes with "hose".)*

JOSIE. It's not a shirt, Porker, it's a blouse. Boys wear shirts, girls wear blouses ... *(Florence re-enters; goes to line sets up for work.)*

FLORENCE. Mornin' ...

JOSIE. I hope you kept your mouth closed when you kissed him!

FLORENCE. You got it: mouth closed, legs open.

RUTHIE. Nice talk! *(Sally re-enters, whisk-broom in hand, sweeps steps to kitchen, vigorously brushing his dirt findings into dustpan. He checks his work, satisfied that steps are spandy clean, goes down steps to handtruck, exits in freezer. Everyone pauses to watch him come, work, go.)*
JOSIE. What's *with* him?
FLORENCE. New government inspector starts today ...
JOSIE. What happened to Haddie?
FLORENCE. She was just a fill in temp ...
JOSIE. No kidding?
PORKER. Abolutely. She was just fillin' in 'til the Feds found a full-time replacement for Dorothy ...
ARLYNE. Poor Dorothy. Hard to believe ...
JOSIE. Hard to believe ...
PORKER. Un-believable ...
RUTHIE. I still can't believe it, myself ... *(Josie and Florence exchange a private glance. Florence breaks the eye-contact; moves U. Sally re-enters with hand-truck. He sets down pallette with crates of frozen product at head of "line", ready for processing.)*
MAUREEN. Mornin', Sal ...
SALLY. Mornin', Reenie ...
JOSIE. *(Pulling sweater off over head.)* Boys, close your eyes!
SALLY. You're supposed to be usin' the big room!
JOSIE. *(Wears lacy bra; "flashes" the men.)* Cheap thrills!
SALLY. Very comical! *(To all.)* I'm tellin' her and I'm tellin' ya's all: you made me set up the big room downstairs with changin' booths and a cot and a Mr. Coffee and bullshit, and if ya's ain't gonna' use all that, I'm gonna' return the merchandise and use the space for something profitable!
JOSIE. Ain't nothin' profitable goin' on around North Shore Fish ...
SALLY. I can use it for storage ...
JOSIE. Keep runnin' the front office the way it's bein' run, you'll be able ta' use the whole plant for *storage!*
SALLY. You wanna' watch that mouth of yours, sis'tah, huh? Jobs are gettin' scarce.

JOSIE. I wonder who we get ta' blame for that particular turn of events, huh?

SALLY. What's this I'm hearin'?

JOSIE. What's yo'r problem, Sally? Waxey ears? You can't hear clear what I'm sayin'? *(Closer; loudly.)* I'm sayin' North Shore Fish is goin' *down the tubes!* *(Sally blanches white, raises the back of his hand as though he might hit Josie. Florence steps between them.)*

FLORENCE. *(Stares him down, eyeball-to-eyeball.)* Stay back from her.)

SALLY. *(Sally puts his hand to his side.)* I'm gonna tell ya's all somethin' straight: This is not the day!

JOSIE. What's your plan for the new Inspector, Sal? You gonna grab her in the freezer for a cold quickie, or are you gonna' go for a long and meaningful relationship? Hmmm?

SALLY. Just watch your ass.

JOSIE. *(She looks down to her derriere.)* Okay, now there are *three* of us watching my ass: me, you, and Hotlips Martino. *(Sally walks to end of "Line", moves blocks of frozen fish into position for processing. He then exits into refrigerator.)*

PORKER. I got that, you know.

JOSIE. Why shouldn't you have got that? Was anybody speakin' in complex sentences you mightn't comprehend? *(To all.)* I'm goin' to the big room to change. I wouldn't wanna' be the cause of Sal bringin' our Mr. Coffee back ta' Zayre's! *(Josie exits. Porker goes to Florence.)*

PORKER. What was the implication s'pose'ta be there? That I'm *stupid* or something?

FLORENCE. That was no implication, Porker. That was a *fact of life!*

PORKER. Me: stupid? I ain't the one callin' no TV-dolphin "Gentle Ben". Gentle Ben was a goddam grizzly bear, you dodo! The TV dolphin for about a hundred years, as everybody know, was "Flipper"! *(To all.)* Right? Is this not right? Is this not a perfectly right fact?

FLORENCE. That wasn't me, ya' nincompoop! I was just goin' along 'counta' I didn't wanna' hurt Arlyne's feelin's. If your memory ain't eaten away by the drugs, you might recall it was Arlyne who come up with Gentle goddam Ben and hardly myself! I said nothin' ... I just went along ...

ARLYNE. *(Eavesdrops; interjects.)* Yuh, I think I did, and you're definitely right, Porker. Gentle Ben was a bear. Flipper was the porpoise ...

FLORENCE. Dolphin ...

RUTHIE. Same thing, if you ask me. They look like big hairy slugs ...

PORKER. What do you mean "slugs"?

RUTHIE. Slugs. Slugs are slugs ...

PORKER. Like in a gun in a gangster movie "slugs"?

FLORENCE. Jesus, what a dork!

PORKER. I'm just askin'! I'm just checkin'!

FLORENCE. She don't mean "slugs" like in a gangster movie. She don't mean "slugs" like after you make a bad smell, neither, dork!

PORKER. Will you get off my goddam case!

RUTHIE. What I mean is slugs like you get when you grow your own lettuce ... in the vegetable garden ... black fleshy hairy slimey disgusting slugs!

FLORENCE. See?

PORKER. I know that!

RUTHIE. Porpoises are like big bloated-up slugs! Used'ta'make me sick when we used'ta go into North Station to Barnum & Bailey's Circus, when I was little ...

PORKER. Porpoises?

FLORENCE. *(Confidentially; to Porker.)* Don't you correct her, you!

PORKER. Did I say nothin' *(He shows his palms to Florence.)*

RUTHIE. *(Continuing; quite disgusted.)* These porpoises would come out (big hairy slimey fleshy things with whiskers) and they'd kinda *flop around* ... all fleshy and slug-like! The trainers would feed 'em live fish, which they'd kinda *suck up,* then they'd bark some kinda' weird kinda' dog-like soundin' bark, and then they toot out something on car horns or somesuch. I usually had my eyes

closed at that point, and had my legs clamped together tight, in case they got loose and came at me, and, you know, tried to get under my skirt or anything ... *(There is a small astonished silence.)*
ARLYNE. Jeffrey once put five or six slugs in Ruthie's underpants to scare her, when she was little. She was about then, maybe eleven ...
RUTHIE. Gawd, Mama, Jesus!
ARLYNE. ...I'm never suppose'ta mention it out loud ...
RUTHIE. Gawd!
ARLYNE. Little boys can be very mean to little girls ... *(There is another small silence. Sally re-enters with a hand-truck with several fresh blocks of frozen fish-product stacked neatly on a pallette, ready for processing.)*
SALLY. What is the *matter* with you people? Do you see the clock? We're just about to have a bell! S'posin' Markie comes in early? No saws on, no batter mixed and ready! A new inspector startin' today and nobody set up ta' work! This is brilliant, people, huh, with what's goin' down here, huh? Huh? Am I talkin' for my own good here, or am I talkin' for the good of all'a ya's, huh? *(Porker walks wordlessly to the band-saw and flips the on-switch "on". Arlyne walks to the wrapping-sealer and flips the on-switch "on". Florence walks to the batter-tank and flips the on-switch "on". Ruthie moves along the "line" to the hot-plastic-wrap station; hits the "on" switch. Josie re-enters with Maureen and Marlena. They re-join the "line" at their various work-stations.)* Where *were* you people? You're not even set up!
JOSIE. We were just givin' the new girl the lay of the land.
PORKER. *(Guffaws.)* You ought'a know! Haggghhh!
JOSIE. What's that noise just come out'ta Porker? Sounded like a trained *seal!* Somebody throw Porker a fish! *(Guffaws.)*
SALLY. Get set up, okay? *(Maureen and Josie exchange a private glance.)*
JOSIE. Sorry I razzed ya', Sal. I know you're feelin' pressured. *(Maureen and Josie exchange another private glance. Maureen smiles approvingly.)*
SALLY. I accept. *(Sally pats Josie's bottom.)* Don't sweat it.
JOSIE. *(Smiles.)* So, how's Carmella and the kid's doin'? Okay? ...

SALLY. Great, great, terrific. *(To Maureen.)* Get your cousin set up, too, okay? This is her ... she ... right? *(Smiles flirtatiously at Marlena.)* We ain't been officially introduced yet. I'm Sal.
MAUREEN. Sorry, Sal. This is Marlena, Sal. Marlena, this is Sal. Sal's foreman.
SALLY. Very pleased ta' meet'cha ...
MARLENA. Likewise ...
SALLY. Maybe we can meet up later and I can show you some tricks ... how ta' handle product kind of thing ... *(Marlena and Sally exchange a flirtatious glance. Florence flashes an angry stare at Sally. To Maureen.)* Get her set up ... *(He exits into office. They all set up to work: get ready for the bell.)*
FLORENCE. What gives here?
MAUREEN. I'm just breakin' Marlena in, so's she can cover for me next month, when Anthony and I are travelin'. She's my cousin ... That there's Florence Rizzo: she batters ...
MARLENA. Hi.
FLORENCE. Hi.
MAUREEN. These two here are Ruthie and her mother, Mrs. Flynn ...
ARLYNE. Arlyne ...
MARLENA. Hi ...
ARLYNE. Hi ...
RUTHIE. Hi ...
MAUREEN. *(To Marlena.)* Get boxes off the stack ... about so many. *(Indicated amount with her hands.)*
MARLENA. *(Enroute to box-supply; to Ruthie.)* How far along are you?
ARLYNE. She's overdue.
RUTHIE. *(Pats her stomach.)* I'm ten months. *(Munches her donut; laughs.)* I'm eating for two.
JOSIE. *(Pats her own stomach.)* I've been eating for two all my *life!* Anybody got any extra food?
ARLYNE. I've got a ricotta pie from Mike's. You hungry already? Didn't you eat breakfast?
JOSIE. A'course I ate breakfast! That's my point. I was just

checking for later. If I eat my lunch, early, around ten/ten thirty, which is my plan, I'll get hungry again around eleven/eleven-thirty ...
ARLYNE. I'll save you half ...
JOSIE. You're the best, Arlyne! Honest ta' God.
RUTHIE. My doctor got my due-date wrong, on account of I'm never regular. I think I probably wasn't even pregnant when I first went in for the check-up, but, we all figured it was a definite, 'counta' I missed two months straight 'n all ... So, Earl and I relaxed our system and next thing I know ...
ARLYNE. *(Completes the sentence.)* Pregnant!
JOSIE. Earl and Ruthie use the Basic Cape Ann Catholic System.
RUTHIE. Oh yuh, what's that?
JOSIE. *(Shrugs; explains simply.)* Getting Pregnant.
RUTHIE. That's about the size of it ...
JOSIE. *What's* about the size of it? *(Reasonably raunchy laugh from all.)* Gloucester men have it down to a science: they drink til about 3 a.m., and then they come in making enough noise to wake all the kids up. Then they roll you over and come, faster than you can say "I ain't got my diaphram in!" Then they drop dead asleep. You miss your period. They get pissed off. They meet young out-of-town girls who take aerobics, and they move out of the house. *(There is a long embarrassed pause.)*
MAUREEN. Josie's goin' through a bad time.
MARLENA. *(Smiles at Ruthie.)* You'll probably deliver soon. You're carrying low.
RUTHIE. I dunno' ...
ARLYNE. She always carries low. I used to carry down around my knees somewhere.
RUTHIE. I got a lot bigger the last two times. I hope you're right. I'd hate to stay pregnant for thirteen or fourteen *months*! Jesus, that'd be *awful!*
PORKER. *(Looks at Marlena admiringly.)* So, this is the cousin, huh?
MARLENA. Yuh. Hi. I'm Marlena ... Reenie's cousin.

MAUREEN. That's Porker. He's on the band saw. I wouldn't walk too close. It could kill you ...
MARLENA. His saw?
FLORENCE. His *breath!* *(The women laugh. Porker is disgusted.)*
MAUREEN. I hope you don't mind Marlena coverin' for me while I'm gone. Keeps the money in the family ...
FLORENCE. I don't mind ...
RUTHIE. It's fine, great, no problem ...
MAUREEN. I checked it out with Markie ...
FLORENCE. Sure, no problem ...
JOSIE. Maureen worried you might be p.o.ed about it, 'count'a yo'r Mum ...
FLORENCE. Naw, what the hell, huh? If Markie okayed it, huh? 'Sides, my Mum's got a million things ta' do. She doesn't miss any of this, I can tell you that ...
JOSIE. Florence's Mum worked here nearly thirty straight years.
MARLENA. Ohhh ...
FLORENCE. Laid her off, a couple of months ago. Bloodless fuckin' people run this place ... *(The work bell rings. Full sound of machines, on tape. All work, feverishly. Sounds fade under, work continues.)*
RUTHIE. Whose side of the family you on?
MARLENA. How's that?
RUTHIE. Maureen's Da's side, or the Mum's?
MARLENA. Oh, neither. I'm Anthony's cousin ...
RUTHIE. Oh, yuh, right ... *(Sal re-enters from office.)*
SALLY. Anybody gonna' pack fish here, or what? *(To Florence.)* Could I see you, private. *Now! (Sal exits into upstage kitchen; Florence follows.)*
MARLENA. Boy, he works ya, huh!
MAUREEN. Yuh, well, business is a little off.
JOSIE. Right! Business is a "little off" and Ruthie is a "little pregnant"!

PORKER. Yuh, well, we can turn it around if we hustle! *(While nobody actually answered Porker in words, they have all now begun their day's labor, and seriously.)*

MAUREEN. You'll be settin' up boxes, like so ... tight corners, like so ... *(Maureen demonstrates setting up a box. Marlena watches, imitates.)*

ARLYNE. They've gotta' be tight and trim.

MAUREEN. *(Smiles; imitates Arlyne.)* Tight and trim.

RUTHIE. Earl says he heard some Boston Mafioso's interested in buyin' Markie out ... *(We now see Sal and Florence, upstairs, in office, through window. They are arguing. Work continues, full tilt.)*

JOSIE. They're fighting again.

RUTHIE. They're either fighting or ... you know ... doin' the opposite.

JOSIE. *(Laughs at Ruthie's euphemism.)* How come Earl's gettin' this secret information about Markie and all? *(Josie smiles at Maureen knowingly.)*

RUTHIE. When Earl was pickin' up here, yesterday, he saw some big muscleman bodyguard Mafioso-type hangin' around Markie's office — fifth day in a row ...

MAUREEN. *(Filling Marlena in.)* Earl's Ruthie's husbin'. He picks up our garbage every night ...

RUTHIE. *(Interjects; corrects, instantly.)* Refuse!* *[Means "trash".]

MAUREEN. *(Smiles, allows herself to be corrected.)* Refuse.

RUTHIE. He seen this humongous bodyguard type hangin' around five days straight ...

PORKER. I seen him myself.

JOSIE. What's this?

PORKER. There's been this muscleman type — like Ruthie says Earl says — a Mafioso bodyguard kind of person ... hangin' out with Markie ...

MAUREEN. *(To Marlena.)* Markie owns the plant ...

JOSIE. Markie Santuro's got a bodyguard?

PORKER. Nobody said that! I just said this big jamoca's be'n hangin' out in the front office ...

JOSIE. What the hell does Markie Santoro need a bodyguard for? This place is gettin' weird! *(NOTE: through office window, we see Florence and Sal are again in a passionate embrace.)* They stopped fighting. now they're back to *(Imitates Ruthie here.)* "...you know... doin' the opposite", again.

PORKER. *(Eyeing the work-load.)* We'd better keep it movin', huh?

MAUREEN. C'mon, Parker! We musta' already packed more this week than we did last whole month! *(To Marlena.)* Everybody's feelin' the pressure ... under-the-gun kind of thing, about the plant bein' in trouble'n all ...

ARLYNE. North Shore Fish was a wonderful place to work, years back ...

MAUREEN. *(To Marlena.)* Arlyne's worked here years and years...

ARLYNE. Use'd'ta be if you got on a line at North Shore Fish, your worries were over ... *(NOTE: At this point in the conversation among the workers, labor should be at fairly brisk pace. It should be obvious that the workers have sped up the normal pace of their normal labor: that there is concern about the possibility of the plant's closing: that all conversation is simultaneous to labor, but, at no time does labor ever stop for conversation. Florence re-enters, goes down the stairs to her machine.)*

FLORENCE. I'm runnin' out'ta bricks, Martino!

PORKER. What are you givin' me here ...

FLORENCE. If this place goes under, it ain't gonna' be *my* fault, I can tell you that! *(She re-stocks the "line".)*

JOSIE. I'm out'ta cartons, Porker.

PORKER. Sure thing, Jose. *(To Florence.)* I'm givin' Josie a hand.

ARLYNE. When my mother first started workin' a line here, it was a very respectful occupation ... kinda' like equal almost to a job a school-educated woman might get. Right up there.

FLORENCE. Hurry it up, Martino! If those blocks melt, the fish'll come back ta' life and they are very pissed off about what we've be'n doin' to 'em, I can tell ya' that!

PORKER. Hold yo'r hosses!

JOSIE. He's helpin' me! *(Sally exits office, hops down stairs, passes through all, inspecting work-progress enroute to freezer. He stops at Marlena, checks her box-making.)*

SALLY. Excellent! *(He touches Marlena's cheek, affectionately, setting up a jealousy; a competitiveness. Everybody looks at them.)* Good looking, and smart, too! *(Florence looks over, annoyed and hurt. Sally exits into freezer; off. Josie and Porker are working together, downstage. The lights shift to them slightly.)*

JOSIE. So, how's Rose and your fatha'?

PORKER. Rose is fine. My fatha's fine.

JOSIE. Good weekend?

PORKER. Yuh, we did stuff. How's about yourself, Jose? Good weekend, too?

JOSIE. Well, you know, it ain't the same ...

PORKER. Cookie's a good guy, really. I'd call this temporary insanity, more'n anything else ...

JOSIE. Yuh, well, I guess ...

PORKER. I guess it's toughest on the kids, huh?

JOSIE. Yuh, well, they know he ain't around, that's for sure. They're fightin' all the time ...

PORKER. Temporary insanity. He'll be back...

JOSIE. Why? You hear anything?

PORKER. Me? No.

JOSIE. You seen them?

PORKER. Together?

JOSIE. Yuh, well, yuh ...

PORKER. Down the Rigger, just the once, last week. And down the Blackburn, a little more recent ...

JOSIE. Saturday night?

PORKER. Yuh, well, yuh ...

JOSIE. Everybody's been tellin' me that. If my fatha' hears, I can't be responsible for what he'll do ...

PORKER. To Cookie?

JOSIE. A'course to Cookie! *(Leans in; confidentially.)* You tell him something for me, Porker. You tell him if my fatha' hears, he's gonna'

cut his balls off and feed 'em to the seagulls ... *(Pauses; nods.)* You tell him that.
PORKER. Anything else?
JOSIE. Yuh. Tell 'im the kids are fine, not to worry. Tell him I'm startin' ta' look around myself, ta' see, you know, who's available and who's unavailable sort of thing ...
PORKER. You want me to *say* that?
JOSIE. Are you my friend or what?
PORKER. Come on, Josie, you know I am, since how many years?
JOSIE. So, you'll tell him?
PORKER. Cookie's my friend, too ...
JOSIE. Who's closer?
PORKER. Well, you know ... we were a thing, you and me. Me and Cookie were never a thing ... *(Josie is aware of everyone eavesdropping, she makes a "public" private statement.)*
JOSIE. When I start doin' it again, with other men, you'll be among the first ...
PORKER. I know that ... *(Leans in to steal a kiss. Josie sees everybody is watching; pulls back.)*
JOSIE. What are you? Crazy? ... *(Florence and Ruthie and Maureen exchange a smile. Maureen resumes explaining the labor to Marlena. The lights re-widen to include all.)*
MAUREEN. It's pretty much like cuttin', only different. *(To Arlyne.)* Marlena used'ta cut, up Essex.
ARLYNE. I used'ta work live fish, myself.
MAUREEN. Smells better workin' live fish.
FLORENCE. Oh, yuh, the batter's a killer ... I think they put formaldehyde in it, to keep the fish lookin' tasty! *(Sally re-enters with palette-truck; he arrives at the end of the "line" with crates of already packaged frozen fish, in individual boxes.)*
SALLY. Porker! Gimme a hand here, Pork ... *(Porker goes to Sally. Together, they stack the individual boxes on the end table.)*
PORKER. Where are these goin'?
SALLY. I dunno', back to Japan. Label's all Japanese. Some Chicago broker called it in ...

PORKER. Crazy goddam thing, huh?
SALLY. What? Sendin' it back ta' Japan? Yuh, well, it's business ... Who cares?
MAUREEN. See how Porker cuts those big blocks down into bricks? The machine is shaping them fish-like and Floey breads them ... you and me set up the boxes, then Ruth and Arlyne box 'em ... and Josie wraps and that's it ...
MARLENA. How come they gotta shape 'em so they're fish-like?
MAUREEN. So, they look like fish. You wouldn't wanna eat a fish that looked like a brick, would ya?
MARLENA. Yuh, but, if they're already fish, how come they're not already *shaped* like fish?
MAUREEN. 'Cause they're really about a million fish all smashed together ...
FLORENCE. It's more like a family of fish than just a fish ... *(Holds up slab of fish.)* See, look close. Piece of a middle, piece of a neck, another piece of middle, little tail ...
MARLENA. Wow, is that ever *gross!*
FLORENCE. It's nothin' compared to the breading ...
MARLENA. Is the fish local?
FLORENCE. God, no. The fish is from Boston, mostly ...
MARLENA. That's where they catch it?
FLORENCE. That's where they buy it. They buy it in auctions, like ... already frozen. Some of it's Canadian, some of it's Japanese. It comes from all over.
MAUREEN. All the *live* fish is local ...
MARLENA. Oh, yuh, I know that ...
PORKER. See these blocks we're cutting up. They're from Japan, 6,000 miles away. All we're doing is cutting them up, spraying a little batter on them and sending them right back to Japan: 12,000 miles round trip. Don't ask me. I only work here.
MARLENA. No kidding? That is *weird* ...
FLORENCE. Your cousin puts notes in the far-away stuff ...
MAUREEN. ... Yuh, well, I do. So what? *(The women laugh at Maureen, affectionately. Maureen checks to see if Sally is listening.)*

Sometimes, if stuff is goin' to, you know, Japan or Australia, someplace really *far*, I like to toss in a couple of words. Nothin' too much ... Maybe "Hi, I'm Maureen Vega from Gloucester, Mass., U.S. of A. I'm thirty-one and I like [Slyvia Plath and] summers." That kind of thing. *(The women continue their labor, as they chat. The fishbricks are moved along to the various stations and the fish is shaped, breaded, wrapped, packed and labeled. Unnoticed at first, at the furthermost end of the room, Catherine Shimma enters. She wears a coat, collar up, high-heeled shoes. She is extremely attractive, far more worldly-looking than the other women. She moves to center, pauses; watches.)*
ARLYNE. I can remember workin' here some years back when we were still cuttin' live fish, we used'ta have two three four Japs standin' lookin' right over our shoulders, makin' bids right then and there, you know, against each other and all ...
MAUREEN. They are great fish-eaters, the Japanese ...
ARLYNE. Oh, you don't have to tell me! I've seen Japs with my own eyes: they have a true respect for fish ... I wish they didn't bomb Pearl Harbor, but, they must have had their reasons. That's all I'm going to tell ya's ...
SALLY. *(Re-enters with hand-truck; sees Shimma.)* Can I help you?
SHIMMA. I'm looking for Salvatore Morella.
FLORENCE. *(In childish schoolgirl sing-song chant.)*
Salll-vaaah-torrr ...
Close-the-doorrrr!
SALLY. *(To Florence.)* What are you? Demented? *(To Shimma.)* I'm him ... he ... this is me: Sal Morella ... Plant Manager ...
FLORENCE. *(Injects.)* Sal M*onilla* ... the disease!
SALLY. ... Who are you?
SHIMMA. Catherine Shimma ...
SALLY. Oh, well, *good. (Sally flashes look of anger at Florence. Everyone has stopped work and is staring at Sally and Florence and Shimma, openly. Sally flashes angry looks to all. He then turns again to Shimma, smiling boyishly.)* Let's go up the front office, and meet Markie. He's the owner. Then I'll show you your kitchen ... *(Shimma walks directly to the breading vat, allows breading to flow on*

to her finger. She tastes the breading. Then she picks up a wedge of frozen fish and breaks it into its component pieces: a few sections of fish-necks, etc. She tosses pieces into tray. Then she looks at Sally; nods. Sally leads her off; she follows.) This way ...
SHIMMA. After you ...
SALLY. No, this way ... After you ...
SHIMMA. No. You first. *(There is a moment of silence.)* Go. *(Sally obeys; leads the way off. They exit. Everyone stares after them; astonished.)*
FLORENCE. She look like anybody?
PORKER. Everybody looks like somebody ...
FLORENCE. I know she looks like *some*body, wiseass. I mean, does she look like anybody we know?
PORKER. Not ta' me ... *(Shrugs.)* She looks kinda', I dunno', *sophisticated* ...
FLORENCE. I dunno' ... She's got somethin' familiar goin' ...
JOSIE. She looks like me, before I discovered the blueberry muffins down the Glass Sailboat. Thinnish, small knockers ... *(She stacks a supply of empty boxes in front of her; continues talking as she continues wrapping frozen breaded fish.)* I dunno' why I bother to put the muffins in my mouth. I ought'a just apply them directly to my hips ...
ARLYNE. *(As she labors.)* You have a nice shape, Josie ...
JOSIE. Yuh, right, so did last year's Dodge Vans. They had a nice shape, too!
MAUREEN. You read that book about the guy who ran Dodge? What's'name ... funny name ... "Coke-head", somethin' odd like that ...
JOSIE. Sounds great.
MAUREEN. No, it was. Different. Interestin', really. All about how they spied on him and all. Made you think.
JOSIE. I'll have to pick it up and read it. *(They labor a while. Suddenly, Maureen calls out.)*
MAUREEN. Iococca!
PORKER. What's with her?
MAUREEN. Name of a book.

PORKER. What kind of book?
JOSIE. Squarish, paper pages, with printing all over 'em ...
PORKER. I love a good joke. I wish somebody would tell me one.
FLORENCE. You *are* one! C'mon, Martino, I'm out'ta batter!
MAUREEN. Fantastic thing, big business, really... *(Porker brings new supply of batter to Florence.)*
PORKER. What are you doin'? Throwing it on the floor?
FLORENCE. When I work, I work ... when I party, I party ... 'cause, that's the kinda' guy I am ... *(She playacts being a man: she scratches her crotch and pretends to spit on the floor.)*
MAUREEN. Iococca took Dodge and turned it around ...
FLORENCE. Whose Dodge?
MAUREEN. The whole company. It was goin' out'ta business. He put it back into profits, almost by himself ...
FLORENCE. He know anything about the fish-business? Maybe we can set him up here, huh? *(Laughs. Porker brings her new supply of bricks [or batter].)*
PORKER. We got no problems here so long as we get the product out. *(Everyone labors more enthusiastically, somehow inspired by Lee Iococca.)*
ARLYNE. North Shore Fish has seen good times and bad times. We survive 'em both.
RUTHIE. Where were you born?
MARLENA. Me? *(Ruthie nods.)* Up Newburyport ... *(Pauses.)* We moved down Burlington, when I was nine, but soon as I was old enough to do it on my own, I moved back on the water.
ARLYNE. Oh, I agree! When you're born on the water, you never can live anyplace else!
RUTHIE. My mother and fatha' broke up over water.
ARLYNE. That wasn't the only reason, but, it was *one* of 'em.
RUTHIE. That's the way you always told it to *me!*
ARLYNE. Well, her father was livin' with, you know, another woman and all ...
RUTHIE. He was workin' up Needham ...
ARLYNE. He took a place up near his plant and wanted me to

move up with him. I couldn't do it... I was 6 months pregnant with Ruthie ...
RUTHIE. My grandmother and grandfather and aunts and all were in town ...
ARLYNE. ... My mother and fatha' were here in Gloucester... my sisters, too. I couldn't just pick up and leave all that! Kids, too ... *(Josie, Florence and Ruthie recite Arlyne's oft-spoken thoughts with her, in unison, lovingly. Arlyne never notices.)*

RUTHIE. His job wasn't permanent.	ARLYNE. His job wasn't permanent...	
FLORENCE. She commuted up weekends.	ARLYNE. I commuted up weekends...	JOSIE. Weekends!
ARLYNE. He wanted me there full-time...		FLORENCE. He wanted her there full-time.
ARLYNE. He took another woman...	RUTHIE. Weekends...	JOSIE. Mondays through Fridays...
ARLYNE. Two-timer! They're all alike!	FLORENCE. They're all alike!	JOSIE. At least, I'm still in Gloucester, on the water.

ARLYNE. At least I'm still in Gloucester, on the water... *(There is a short silence.)*
RUTHIE. We live out on the Fort ...
MAUREEN. Ruthie and Earl live upstairs, over Arlyne.
MARLENA. Can you see the water?
RUTHIE. Oh, God, No! We face in, over the freezer plant. But, we can drive over to Good Harbor Beach in — what? — ten minutes. A'course, you gotta' go at *night!*
MAUREEN. Traffic's wicked, summ'ah'time ... during beach hours ...
FLORENCE. I tried to get there, day before yesterday, on our lunch-break ...
MAUREEN. *(Smiles.)* I remember ...
FLORENCE. I never fuckin' made it ... *(Politely.)* Sorry, Arlyne ...

ARLYNE. I don't mind. I know you're angry...

FLORENCE. Two million summah people, one to a car. I dunno why the hell they don't just *team up?* I mean, *none* of us got there! We just sat on Bass Avenue maybe thirty-five minutes I turned around. Took shit from Markie for bein' late comin' back, too...

MAUREEN. We all ask "How's the beach?" 'cause we all figure Floey's beet-red from laying out in the sun. A' course she's beet-red with a fever and all from sittin' in her car in traffic on Bass Ave! *(Sally and Shimma exit front office and enter kitchen, closing door behind them. Sally makes "Keep it down" signal to all before closing door. Porker slides upstage, plants himself under window to kitchen in order to spy on Sally and Shimma, inside.)*

FLORENCE. This new one ain't gonna' buy his greaseball charm, I can tell ya's all *that!*

MAUREEN. If our product's good, what's the diff? She's not inspectin' Sal, she's inspectin' product, right?

FLORENCE. Yuh, so, if that's true, what's he tryin' ta' get into her pants for? Answer me that?

RUTHIE. Nice talk, huh ...

FLORENCE. Yuh, well, I'm just not up for bein' out'ta work all next year, that's all ...

PORKER. Come on, Florence. Sal can handle this ... I'm gonna' watch closer. *(Porker moves upstage; spies on Sally.)*

MARLENA. What's she sayin', Maureen?

MAUREEN. Florence is a little negative, on account'a this and that.

MARLENA. Which and what?

FLORENCE. I heard that, Reenie. I ain't a "little negative". I am *very fucking negative!* Look around you! You see how empty it is here? This place looks like a fortune cookie, after somebody took the message! There's nobody here, Reenie! This is a dead place. The fish business has had it! *Absolutely definitely had it!*

ARLYNE. Florence Marie Rizzo, you close that mouth!

FLORENCE. *(Sincerely; childlike.)* Sorry, Arlyne ...

ARLYNE. What if your mother heard you ... ?

FLORENCE. I know ...

ARLYNE. Businesses have ups and downs ...
FLORENCE. It's true ...
ARLYNE. The fish business just has fewer ups and more downs, that's all ...
FLORENCE. I suppose ...
ARLYNE. We are fish people. We are doing what we were born to do ...
FLORENCE. I don't think that ... *(Thinks better of it.)* I guess ... *(Florence and Ruthie and Arlyne, in unison, complete Arlyne's oft-spoken thoughts.)*
ARLYNE & OTHERS. "Negative criticism will only bring the very thing you dread right down onto your head ..." *(Florence smiles at Ruthie, gratefully.)*
ARLYNE. That's what my mother used ta' say ta' me, and she was right. That's all I'm gonna' tell ya's ... *(Ruthie and Florence exchange another conspiratorial glance and smile.)* She was a smart woman, my mother. We worked together ...

ARLYNE. ... elbow to elbow, side by...	ALL OTHERS. ... elbow to elbow, side by side...

ARLYNE. *(Alone.)* It's a wonderful thing when you can earn your livin' workin' side-by-side with people who care about you...
FLORENCE. I know ... *(Florence moves upstage with empty stock-tray, which she will replace with full stock-tray.)*
ARLYNE. And it's a wonderful thing to live your life overlookin' the water.
MARLENA. Oh, I agree. There's something so special about livin' on the water ...
RUTHIE. Definitely! The water gets in yo'r blood ...
MARLENA. ... Takin' walks on the shore ...
FLORENCE. My fatha' used'ta be able ta' name all the flowers over Braces' Cove ... Dropwort Shoots and so forth ... Angelica and stuff. You'd think you were hearin' some kind of Ha'vid professor, honest ta' God! *(We see Sally, above, in office, touch Shimma's cheek. Florence sees as well. Shimma pulls back, angrily.)* Ah, shit ...
RUTHIE. That's the thing: knowing you know everything about the ocean, because you've lived your life on it ... Naming all the fish

right. That sort'a thing ...

MAUREEN. I like thinkin' about what's out there ... across from us ...

JOSIE. I got enough trouble thinkin' about what's right under my nose ... *(Eats a Snickers bar.)* Oh, God, I ate it! I was gonna' save that for afta' lunch!

MAUREEN. You know, if you go straight out from here across the northern part of England, there isn't a single mountain range between us and the Ural Mountains in Russia ...

MARLENA. Is that right?   JOSIE. No kidding?

MAUREEN. If you could blow hard enough, you could blow out somebody's birthday candles in Russia, and that is a fact ... *(Shimma is clearly annoyed with Sally.)*

PORKER. I think they're fighting ...

FLORENCE. You say something?

PORKER. I think Sally's yellin' at the new inspector ... *(They all turn and look. Sally storms out of the kitchen, slamming the door. He runs down the stairs. Each worker busies herself with her labor. Sally moves directly to the refrigerator, about to exit. He stops, thinks better of it; talks.)*

SALLY. I want every fifth fillettee weighed. I want no light product. And check the batter. I want no thick breading. If this bull-dyke wants to play it by the rules, I say "fine"! I say we give her perfect product and let her break her own dyke balls and if anybody here says different, let them bread their own ass too thick and find work elsewhere, 'cause this plant is not goin' under! *(And with that, Sally exits into the freezer. After a pause, he re-enters.)* Porker, I want sixty crates of the Howard Johnson's out and ready to rewrap with Stop'n'Shop!

PORKER. That order ain't due for three and a half weeks ...

SALLY. I give *no shit!* The second that vicious mother of a bitch rejects one miserable underweight or triple-breaded fillette, we go off the fresh-frozen and right the fuck on to re-wraps. *Bang! (Punches crate, violently.)* I got Stop'n'Shop rewraps, I got Jap re-wraps, I got next year's Daitch-*Shopwell* rewraps. I do not give-a-shit. Is this okay?

PORKER. It's okay.
RUTHIE. It's okay.
MAUREEN. Okay ...   JOSIE. Okay ...
SALLY. I apologize sincerely for my filthy mouth, Arlyne, but, as you can see, I am overwrought ...
ARLYNE. That's no excuse ...
SALLY. Arlyne!
ARLYNE. "A filthy mouth speaks the thought of a filthy mind!"
SALLY. *(Head down, he "mouthes" precise sentence with Arlyne in unison.)* "... of a filthy mind ..." *(He goes to Arlyne.)* Arlyne, we have trouble here! I think I have to warn nobody. I think you can see from the three closed-down lines and the many laid-off close friends and loved ones, this plant is on no solid ground and should she fuck us over, we could go down if not under. *(He spots Shimma walking down staircase from her office.)* Here she comes! *(He runs into freezer. Shimma walks to "Line", carrying a tray; wordlessly. She smiles at everyone, officiously. She places six samples of breaded fish on her tray. Shimma purposefully exits the "Line" area, and re-enters her kitchen. Sally peeks out from behind the freezer door.)* What I smell here is not good ... Porker, come here ... *(To Porker.)* I'm goin' in to Markie. Any kind of move at all: report. You follow me?
PORKER. Yuh, sure ...
SALLY. What'd I say?
PORKER. I got you ...
SALLY. *What'd I say?*
PORKER. I'll get you ...
SALLY. Martino, I am in no fucking *mood!*
PORKER. You're in with Markie. If she makes a move, I'll come get you ...
SALLY. No, this is exactly what I do not want! *(Moves to Porker.)* You know Markie's position here, which I am laboring to change, yes?
PORKER. I have a good idea, yuh ...
SALLY. What the fuck do you mean "I have a good idea, yuh"? I *told* you exactly what his position is on this, right?

PORKER. *(Looks around; worried.)* Yuh, well, shhh, yuh, okay, Sal ...
SALLY. If she makes a negative move or a rejection-like move involving product, this is what you come get me for ... But don't ...
PORKER. *(Finishes the sentence.)* ... let on to Markie!
SALLY. *Exact! (He realizes that Everyone stands, staring.)* Hello? Are you being paid to work, or is this the company clambake, huh, people? Thannnkk youuuuu! *(Everybody starts working again. Sally looks up at Shimma, through window. He then looks over at Porker; exits. Through the window, we can see Shimma, in her office/kitchen, cooking the frozen fish in a microwave oven. She opens the oven, takes out a filet of cooked fish, replaces it with a filet of frozen fish, shuts oven, hits "ON" switch. She weighs cooked fish. She tastes cooked fish, chews it awhile, spits what has been in her mouth into a plastic-bag-lined garbage container; begins to write a report.)*
MARLENA. Look, Reenie, she's eating our fish!
MAUREEN. That's how they do the test: they cook it up and taste it ...
MARLENA. Hey! She spit it out!
JOSIE. They always spit it out ... They taste maybe eighty, ninety pieces of fish a day. Imagine what they'd weigh if they didn't spit it out? I never spit it out. I swallow everything.
PORKER. *Everything?*
JOSIE. You're an embarrassment to the Italian race, you know that? *[NOTE: If actor playing Porker is fat, Josie's line changes to "You're an embarrassment to fat people! You know that?"]*
MARLENA. What if she rejects it ... the fish?
RUTHIE. We have to throw out the batch...
ARLYNE. ... Clean the breader, make new batter...
JOSIE. That's what Dotty did...
ARLYNE. Poor soul...
JOSIE. She was rejecting everything, at the end...
MARLENA. Who's Dotty?
FLORENCE. Dorothy Fabiano. She was Government inspector here for seven years, nearly eight ...

MARLENA. She quit?
MAUREEN. She was the one I was tellin' you about ...
MARLENA. Oh ...
FLORENCE. She died ... She was having a serious thing with Sal for the last four years or so ...
JOSIE. Then, Sal got interested elsewhere ...
FLORENCE. What's this, you?
JOSIE. Just talkin' ...
RUTHIE. Sal's married ... and he got Dot pregnant ...
MARLENA. Reenie was tellin' me ...
FLORENCE. The way people around here see it, Sal was the definite cause of Dot's dyin' ...
ARLYNE. *(Shocked.)* Florence Marie Rizzo, I am not going to let you incriminate Sal so viciously. We are all Catholics here, mostly, and this sort of incrimination is hardly the way we were taught!
FLORENCE. I'm entitled to my opinions, Arlyne. Even though you're Ruthie's mother, I am ... *(Porker and Florence exchange a glance. Porker shakes his head in disgust. Florence returns to her battering.)* I'll stay out of it ...
JOSIE. For the last couple of months or so, Dotty'd wait 'til we get set up with a fresh batch of batter, then she'd come out, get a fish, cook it, shake her head, come out and put her thumb down. No words, nothin', just her thumb down. Sally used'ta' fuckin' *burn* ... *(Laughs.)* Sorry, Arlyne ...
ARLYNE. I know it's something that angers us all ... *(Pauses.)* Dorothy was a lovely, lovely, lovely girl ... Local, too. We all knew her family ... motha', two brothers, sis'tah. Her sistah's teachin' up at O'Malley School right today. Very lovely family, honest ta' God ...
PORKER. She's comin' out! *(Shimma enters; looks about; speaks to Porker.)*
SHIMMA. Where is he?
PORKER. Front office.
SHIMMA. Get him. *(Porker pauses a moment; then runs to door to Markie's office; exits. Shimma looks at Florence and others.)* Beautiful day out there. Beach weather. shame to be trapped inside ...

JOSIE. Ain't I seen you drivin' around town with the "GOLF" license-plate?
SHIMMA. Oh, yuh, that's me, yuh ...
FLORENCE. What's this? You live local or something?
SHIMMA. Oh, no. I live up Woburn.
FLORENCE. Oh, yuh? Woob'in? *(To all; sarcastically.)* Figures.
SHIMMA. Why? You got somethin' against Woburn?
FLORENCE. Me? Naw. So long as I don't hav'ta' drink the water ...
JOSIE. She's got a plate with "GOLF" on it.
SHIMMA. I do, yuh ...
MAUREEN. There's a blue Duster out in the lot with "GOLF" on it!
JOSIE. That's *her.*
SHIMMA. That's me.
MAUREEN. You play golf?
SHIMMA. Me? Uh uh. It's my husbin's plate. It's mine, now, but, it *was* his ...
FLORENCE. Don't I know you?
RUTHIE. *What?*
FLORENCE. I'm not talkin' to *you,* Ruthie, I'm talkin' to the new inspector: her. *(Steps toward Shimma.)* You look wicked familiar to me.
SHIMMA. We met. My husb'in's got cousins who are yo'r husb'in's cousins. He told me ta ask after you when I sta'hted out this mornin' ...
FLORENCE. Is that a fact?
RUTHIE. She's Floey's Cousin! See? You never know ...
JOSIE. You *always* know! Everybody's related to everybody else around these parts. We're even cousins, distant, right, Arlyne?
ARLYNE. I don't think so ...
JOSIE. Aren't you related to the Asaroes?
ARLYNE. No, that's Florence.
FLORENCE. That's me, cupie doll.
JOSIE. If there's anything I hate more than bein' fat, it's bein'

wrong! (To Shimma.) So, how come you got "GOLF" on your plate? Yo'r husb'in some kind'a big golfer?
SHIMMA. My husb'in? Uh uh. He's never played any golf ... *(There is a pause.)* I got him a vanity plate for his birthday and it came through with "GOLF" on it ...
JOSIE. You didn't ask for "GOLF"?
SHIMMA. Not really. There was a bunch'a spaces for choices ... I asked for "Billy", first, on accounta' that's his name; then "Bill"; then "Willy" ... his brother used'ta call him "Willy" ... but, then, there was this fourth empty space for a choice. I shoulda' thought ta' put down "William" but nobody ever calls him that and I guess I forgot that was in the runnin', even. I used'ta drive by this golf club every day when I worked over Wakefield ...
RUTHIE. Bear Hill ...
SHIMMA. That's the one, yuh. I always thought it would be really — I dunno' — sophisticated if he took up golf, so, I just wrote it in in the empty space. I guess "Billy", "Bill" and "Willy" were taken and when the plate came through I got fuckin' "GOLF"! *(She laughs embarrassedly.)*
MAUREEN. He doesn't *ever* play golf, your husb'in?
SHIMMA. Naw, never, no sports at all. He used'ta bowl before I met him ...
JOSIE. Didn't he get pissed off, when you gave 'im the plate?
SHIMMA. Oh, yuh, *wick'id!* That's why *I'm* drivin' the car. He won't *touch* the thing! *(Sally runs into room, followed by Porker. Sally doesn't see Shimma at first, as she is among the workers.)*
SALLY. Where is this dyke?
PORKER. *(Sees.)* Oh, my God ...
SALLY. *(Sees. His attitude changes entirely. He smiles seductively.)* Alfred came got me. You sent him? *(Motions to Porker.)* Him. *(Shimma stares wordlessly at Sally.)* So? What's up? *(Sally smiles his most boyish smile at Shimma.)*
FLORENCE. *(Disgusted.)* Jesus! *(Shimma walks silently into her kitchen; leaves door open. Sally looks around at the women.)*
SALLY. What gives? What were you jawin' about with her? *(He looks them over, one by one.)* We got a plant ta' protect here, ya'

know, so's don't any of ya's play it too *sma'ht*, if you're able ta' got my point ...

FLORENCE. A good couple'a us have *had* your point, Salvatore! It don't look like it's gonna work with this one! *(Motions toward Shimma.)* You might hav'ta use yo'r *brain* for change, ladykiller. *(Sally walks to Florence, slowly, angrily. He stares at her a moment, silently, then turns, moves up staircase to kitchen, tentatively. He then enters kitchen, closing door behind him. We can now see Shimma and Sally in conversation. Porker moves to Florence, subtly; silently. When next to her, he speaks quietly.)*

PORKER. What's the matter with you?

FLORENCE. *(Choking back anger.)* Fuck off ...

PORKER. You lookin' to get smacked, or what?

FLORENCE. *(Angrily.)* Leave me alone ... *(Turns upstage; moves off from others, alone. She paces; angrily; enraged.)*

JOSIE. What'd you say to her, Porker?

PORKER. Oh, yuh, sure ... *me!*

ARLYNE. Just leave her be. Let her collect herself ... That's the best.

RUTHIE. It's embarrassing when you cry ...

ARLYNE. It's better to stand off, alone, get a grip ...

RUTHIE. Collect yo'rself ... *(Pauses; Florence paces like a caged cat upstage.)* Get a grip ... *(Pauses; Florence continues to pace.)* Stand off, alone ... It's embarrassing when you cry ... *(Marlena looks to Maureen for an explanation. Maureen speaks to Marlena quietly, but, certainly not discreetly.)*

MAUREEN. Florence and Sally there are on-again/off-again kind of thing ...

MARLENA. Oh, yuh? Her, too?

JOSIE. Italian men are the worst ...

MAUREEN. Italians, "Portegees", Irish and English: the worst!

RUTHIE. I'd say Jews were the best.

JOSIE. You've never *seen* a Jew!

RUTHIE. I know Mr. Linsky ...

JOSIE. I mean a young Jew: a Jew under thirty ...

RUTHIE. Oh, no, I don't know anybody like that.
JOSIE. *(Smiles.)* Mr. Linsky must be seventy-five ...
ARLYNE. *Sixty*-five ...
MAUREEN. Everybody's nice when they hit sixty-five. They get kinda' *beaten into it!*
ARLYNE. I wouldn't say Linsky's so nice ... *(They all look at Arlyne.)* I could tell you a couple'a stories about Linsky! *(They all smile, enjoying their game.)*
RUTHIE. *(The widest smile of all.)* She's still mad at him over something.
ARLYNE. It ain't money, neither!
RUTHIE. She went out with him once ...
ARLYNE. I wouldn't get too close to Jews if I were you!
RUTHIE. I always bring it up ta' get her goat ...
ARLYNE. Jews are loose with their hands! That's all I'm gonna tell ya's ...
RUTHIE. *(Giggles.)* Never fails me ...
ARLYNE. They can sweet-talk you, all right, but, when push comes to shove, stay clear of Jews. That's all I'm gonna tell ya's ...
RUTHIE. *(Imitating her mother's voice.)* They can break yo'r heart, too ...
ARLYNE. *(Exact same voice, but, tearfully.)* They can break yo'r heart, too ...
RUTHIE. *(Giggles.)* Never fails me! *(Sally and Shimma argue, in kitchen, upstairs. Florence paces away, upstage, alone. She is extremely upset. She watches Sally and Shimma, through kitchen's window-wall, above.)*
JOSIE. So, that rules out Jews, Italians, Portegees, Irish, English ... What's left?
MAUREEN. Frenchmen.
MARLENA. Frenchmen?! You soft in the head? Frenchmen'll fuck *lobsters* if you hold their claws open! Frenchmen are the *worst!*
MAUREEN. How about Frenchmen from Montreal, or from up Vermont? How do you feel on *them?*

MARLENA. That's what I'm *tellin'* ya's! *(Pauses.)* We had a shed built once. Six Frenchmen, all brothers. *(Pauses.)* My husband's upstairs, shavin'. One of the Frenchmen asks me if he can use the downstairs toilet. Another one wants a glass of water. He has his own *glass!* — (I shoulda' known something funny was comin', right?) — I'm in my housecoat still, 'counta' it's maybe 6:30, 6:40 ...
RUTHIE. In the mornin'?
MARLENA. A'course in the mornin'! My husband only shaves in the mornin'! *(Takes a breath.)* The one with his own glass comes up behind me and like presses himself against me. The older one — with the muscle-shirt — he presses himself against me, in front, kisses me. The younger one reaches under and up, around front ...
MAUREEN. *(Interjects.)* You are *kidding* with this!
MARLENA. ... and I, of course, cannot make a *peep* ...
MAUREEN. ... 'cause'a Frank ...
MARLENA. ... 'cause my husband's upstairs, shavin', not thirty feet away. *(Pauses; then smugly.)* So, you wanna' tell me about Frenchmen? *(There is a long astonished pause. Porker is first to break the silence.)*
PORKER. So, what did you do? *(They all look at Porker, as if surprised by his participation.)*
MARLENA. I didn't know he was listenin' ...
JOSIE. Jesus, Porker, you got no *shame? (To Marlena.)* Porker's a tell-me-a-story freak.
PORKER. I wasn't listenin' ... *(To Marlena.)* I wasn't listenin' ... *(To all.)* We need more bricks! (Porker goes to saw; saws down blocks into smaller brick shapes. The women continue their labor, wordlessly. After a while, Maureen talks to Marlena.)*
MAUREEN. You ever tell Frank? *(We become aware again of Florence, upstage, stopped now, watching Sally and Shimma in kitchen-office, through window. Sally touches Shimma's cheek again. Shimma slaps Sally's hand.)*
MARLENA. You kiddin' me? I'd hav'ta have been lookin' to get beat black and blue. *(There is another flurry of wordless work. Josie*

breaks through.)
JOSIE. So, what did they do? *(Marlena looks at Josie.)* The Frenchmen ...
ARLYNE. Josephine!
RUTHIE. Jees, Josie ...
JOSIE. *Why?* Am I the only one interested?
MARLENA. They just kinda groped around for a while and then they left ...
JOSIE. That's it?   RUTHIE. That's all?
(Marlena shrugs, shows her palms. Porker cannot resist a question.)
PORKER. Did you pay 'em? *(Marlena and all look at Porker. He explains quickly.)* For the shed ...
JOSIE. What is *with* you, Porker?
PORKER. It's just a question, that's all! I'm just interested! *(Marlena is done with her story, done talking on the subject. Porker shrugs, shows his palms, sets stack of bricks in front of Florence, at breading machine. Florence is back at work, but still not in commune with the others.)*
JOSIE. Porker forgets from time-to-time. He thinks he's one of *us.*
MAUREEN. They say that dogs do that. Somebody dies in a house, the dog gets depressed. Divorce, too, does the same thing. I read that ... *(Sally storms out of the kitchen, swaggers down stair-case. He is in a rage.)*
SALLY. Burn the crop! Dump it all! I don't want no arguments here, just dump the whole batch! Porker, I want all the HoJo crates ... all of 'em ... *(Screams at Porker.) MOVE!* *(To Arlyne.)* Get the Stop'n'Shop labels, Arlyne, and I want ya's all ta' hear this: the only way this plant's stayin' open is if we can cover our asses for this loss and the losses for the last four months, and even then I'm promisin' nobody nothin' ... except for that leaky douche-bag, who I am promisin' that I will process no fish whatsoever, if that's the way she wants it. I will find orders on rewraps and rewraps only. And if she wants ta' turn down our rewraps, she can sue the Federal Inspector who approved 'em in their last wrap, 'cause they are all approved, all registered, and I don't care if we spend the rest of our lives takin'

Howard fucking Johnson labels off a fish and puttin' Stop'n'fuckin' Shop labels *onta'* fish ... if that's what she's lookin' for, that's what she's gonna' find ... 'cause I say "fuck the dyke!" ... and what I say *goes! (Screams at Porker.) MOVE! (To all.)* You all heard me: dump the product, clean the breader. I ain't havin' her fault us on no fuckin' cleanliness ...
ARLYNE. Is she going to test you on *language*, Salvatore ...
SALLY. Oh, gimme a fffff ... a *break*, Arlyne, will ya'! You *see* what I'm goin' through here?
ARLYNE. This is not an excuse!
SALLY. Ar*lyyyyynnnnne!*
ARLYNE. Out of memory for your mother ...
SALLY. *(To Ruthie. He knows he's beaten.)* Will you talk to her?
RUTHIE. Just say you're sorry. What's the big deal?
SALLY. *(Angrily.)* For the love of Christ, Ruthie, I ... *Okay!* All right! Fine! *(Sweetly, head down, like a four year old boy.)* Arlyne, I'm sorry I swore so much. Okay?
ARLYNE. I understand there's a terrible problem, but, does foul language help anything ...
SALLY. No, but it helps *me!* It makes me feel a little better.
ARLYNE. Do you work alone?
SALLY. *(Still a boy.)* No ... *(Raises his head and attitude, slightly.)* Come *onn*, Arlyne, we are in trouble here!
ARLYNE. *Salvatore!*
SALLY. *(Head down again.)* Okay, okay. I said I was sorry. *(To Ruthie.)* Tell her! Didn't you hear me tell her I was sorry? Didn't I?
ARLYNE. I accept. *(Arlyne offers her cheek for Sal to kiss. He does, head still down. Arlyne kisses Sal's cheek. All is forgiven.)*
SALLY. *(Regains the old manly control.)* Get set up ... all'a'ya's!
JOSIE. Good for you, Arlyne.
RUTHIE. My motha' is *tough!*
ARLYNE. You have to stand your ground. You have to stand up to them. You can't let them get an edge.
RUTHIE. She's known him since the crib. *(Sally is humiliated. He*

storms into Locker area, where Florence stands, smoking a cigarette.)
SALLY. Get out here and pull your part of the load! What da'ya' think you are: *special?* I told ya' ta' lay off a me today, didn't I? I told you I had enough pressure on my head without your bullshit, didn't I? But, could you back off? Nooooo! Could you give me a break for even *one measley day? Nooooooooo.* And I'm s'pose'ta'take you serious when you ask me ta' think about what you're askin' me ta' think about? What are you: off yo'r gourd? *(Sally storms off, to freezer, screaming for Porker.)* Yo, Martino! You partying in there? What's up? *(Sally enters freezer, slamming door closed behind him. All eyes on Florence, who exits locker-area and moves to "line." Suddenly, Florence starts flinging frozen fish sticks about the room, furiously, in a rage. Some of the fish-sticks clunk against the kitchen-office window, causing Shimma to stand and look down, frightened.)*
FLORENCE. I've had it! I have fucking *had it!!!*
JOSIE. Hey, Floey ...
FLORENCE. *(Dumps breading onto the floor, making a horrendous, disgusting mess.)* Fucking men!
MAUREEN. Hey, Flo, come onnn ...
ARLYNE. Florence ...
RUTHIE. Floey, heyyy ... *(Florence knocks one of the tables over. Porker and Sally enter, pushing handtrucks with crates of already wrapped/labeled frozen fish. They see Florence and stop in their tracks.)*
SALLY. You'd better do something ...
PORKER. Me? Shitt ... *(Porker runs to Florence and she beans hiim with a breaded frozen fish-brick.)* Heyy, you tryin' ta' kill me, or what?
FLORENCE. LEAVE ... ME ... ALONE! *(Florence paces, trapped, caged.)*
SALLY. What the hell gives here? Did you do this, Rizzo?
FLORENCE. *(To Porker, about Sally.)* Just keep him the fuck away from me!
PORKER. Just let her calm down a little, Sal ... *(Sally cannot believe his eyes; rages at Florence.)*
SALLY. What are you? *Warped?* With a new inspector around?

You make this mess? What are you? Flipped out? You need a strait jacket, or what? You want me ta' call down ta' Danvers ... have 'em bring the nut-wagon over? Or what? *(Florence charges at Sally, slapping him, scratching him, kicking him. Sally does nothing offensively. He ducks her punches, absorbs her slaps; twists out from under her scratches, dances away from her kicks. For him, it is all accomplished quite easily. He giggles and guffaws, childishly, cruelly.)*

FLORENCE. I'll kill you ... I'll kill you...

SALLY. Look at her! Look at this one! What? You wanna' kick me? You wanna' scratch my eyes out? C'mon, c'monnn ... what's you'r trouble, huh? Come onnn, dooo ittt...

ALL OTHERS. *(Call to them.)*

—Hey, Floey...

—Knock it off, you two...

—Grab Florence...

—Poor kid...

—Do somethin', Porker!

—Grab her, Porker!

FLORENCE. *(Screams, suddenly.)* Fuckin' coward ... hitting women ... beatin' women ... murderer ... Everybody knows ... everybody knows... murderer! *(During the fight, Shimma has quietly exited the kitchen and entered the main work area, standing upstage, watching. Sally stops his giggling on Florence's final "Murderer!" and grabs the now-hysterical Florence by the throat with his left hand, and he raises his right hand, poised to strike Florence. Porker screams at Sally.)*

PORKER. *Hold it, Sal! HOLD IT!*

SALLY. What, Martino, what? You don't want me ta' hit your girlfriend? You don't think I should make over her face? What?

PORKER. You're bein' observed... *(He nods towards Shimma.)*

SALLY. What? *(Looks, sees Shimma; snarls at her.)* What are *you* starin' at? This is a private matter. This is company business... *(Shimma stares at him, silently. Sally releases Florence, shoving her away from him.)* You're free, you... *(Florence circles the plant floor, still in a rage. Animal-like moans issuing from her: deep-throated, primal. Sally goes to Porker and "sucker-punches" him in the stomach;*

hurting him, humiliating him.) That's for your girlfriend, you... *(Porker skids and falls in a crumpled, humiliated heap.)* Get back to work! Get set up for re-wraps! *Hustle!* You're all gettin' paid, *yes? (The women restart their labor in near-robot fashion, mechanically, automatically. Their eyes meet, one by one. Sally is deeply ashamed and embarrassed, but unable to apologize. He cleans some of the mess. Suddenly, Sally screams at Shimma.)* You won't close us down, sister! No matter how much you shove, North Shore Fish is stayin' on its feet... *(To the Women.)* I'll bring the product out... *(To Porker.)* Get up and gimme a hand, you!

(Porker stands, silently. He starts toward Sally after flashing a look at Florence, who stands facing Sally, her body heaving a silent sob every tenth count, as does a child after a tantrum. Sally yells at Florence, through clenched teeth, pointing his finger.) If you ever, *ever*, come at me again, I'll... *(He doesn't complete his sentence. He moves to the freezer.)* I'm getting the product. Get set up... *(To Porker.)* You comin', or what? *(Porker moves to Sally, wordlessly. He is embarrassed, beaten into humiliation, hangdog. Sally and Porker exit into the freezer. There is silence, but for Florence's sharp sobbing intakes of breath: her post-tantrum gasps for oxygen. Shimma is shaken. She holds back her tears; makes pronouncement, to women on the "Line".)*

SHIMMA. You tell that blow'ah I ain't passin' no fuckin' inferior product for *noooooooobody*. You tell him I got people lookin' over my shoulder... and I'm coverin' my own ass, no matter what. Even if I have ta' close this plant down. If I hav'ta, I hav'ta! I'm just doin' a job. You get my point here? *(All nod understanding.)* You tell that blow'ah what I just spoke ... *(Shimma turns, exits into kitchen, slamming door closed behind her. After the doorslam, there is a small silence. We see Shimma, through the window. She sits in chair, bows her head, extemely upset. The women watch her a moment, then look at one another, gravely concerned. Arlyne cocks her head. She is worried.)*

THE LIGHTS FADE TO BLACK.

END OF ACT ONE.

ACT TWO
Scene One

Lights out in the auditorium. In darkness, we hear the sound of a radio playing: a song such as Willie Nelson singing "All Right Woman, All Right Man."*

Lights up in plant. Five hours later. The Women are squashed together on either side of the end of the processing "line", at the wrapping table. They are all involved in the unwrapping and rewrapping of frozen fish dinners: boxed. At the moment, they are stripping the boxes of their "A&P" labels, and rewrapping the boxes with "Good Deal Market" labels.

Neither Porker nor Sally is on stage. Shimma is in her kitchen, at the typewriter, writing reports.

The women sing along with the song. Porker and Sally enter, wheeling handtrucks loaded with fish product in crates. The women are all singing full-voiced, wholeheartedly. Porker and Sally stop, astonished, as they head toward a big finish. Shimma hears Sally, looks up and out, as Sally switches radio "off".

SALLY. What's up? What gives here? We workin' or we partyin', huh? We got a plant fallin' apart here and what are you all doing'? Singin'? This is very bright, very *swift!*

*See special note on copyright page.

JOSIE. C'mon, Sally, we've been singin' all afternoon and we still wrapped sixty crates of Stop & Shop.
SALLY. I just walked in here and half of you wasn't doing a single stick of work.
RUTHIE. We're almost finished, Sal.
PORKER. Maybe if they just played it and didn't sing along?
SALLY. *(Turns on Porker cruelly.)* What is this I'm hearin' now?
PORKER. *(Shows Sally his palms.)* Just an idea ...
SALLY. You wanna come in to Markie with me and maybe take it up with him? *(Pretends to be Porker talking to the boss.)* "Markie, I know we're goin' out'ta business and all, and I know we got a new inspector turnin' down every piece 'a product we process and you're probably gonna' hav'ta' sell the building and the land and all, but, couldn't the girls just have some music ta' listen to, instead of doin' their last couple'a days of paid work? *Hmmmmmmmm?*"
PORKER. *(Interjected into above speech.)* Right, okay... Okay, Sal ... Okay, we'll drop the playin'-music idea ...
SALLY. What have you got? Some private income?
PORKER. Okay, okay, you made your point ...
SALLY. I don't hear an answer to my question, Martino!
PORKER. C'mon, Sal, enough, huh?
SALLY. I would like to hear an answer to my question, Martino!
PORKER. C'mon, Sal, will you?
SALLY. I would like to hear an answer to my question, Martino ...
PORKER. Come onn, Sal, a joke's a joke, huh!
SALLY. I said that I would like an answer to my question. Did you not hear me?
PORKER. Okay, fine. What's your question? *(The women all stand silently watching.)*
SALLY. Do you have a private income?
PORKER. No, Sally, I don't. I don't have a private income. *(Porker is humiliated; head down. Florence walks to radio, switches it back on. James Taylor's "Fire and Rain", blares out.* Sally turns and*

---

* See special note on copyright page.

faces Florence.)
SALLY. What's this? *(There is an enormous tension now in the plant. Sally moves to Florence, who stands her ground, defiantly, sings along with the music for a few beats. The music continues on, but without Florence, now, who stands her ground, silently staring at Sally. There is a long "hold". Sally talks to Porker, without ever breaking his stare at Florence.)* Turn it off. Martino, turn off the radio.
PORKER. Hey, Sally, will ya' ..
SALLY. You workin' for North Shore Fish or what?
PORKER. I'm workin' ...
SALLY. Turn it off. *(After a long, tense pause, Porker heads toward the radio. As he passes Florence, they share a moment. He cannot find the strength she wants him to find: He goes to the radio; switchs it "off". Whilst looking at his shoes, Porker speaks.)*
PORKER. I'll be right back. I gotta' go to the bathroon ... *(Porker exits upstage, out of sight-lines. There is another moment's pause. Sally feels he has won; Florence absorbs Porker's small defeat.)*
SALLY. I called the broker, myself. We can move now on the rewrap jop for A&P ... eighty thousand units. Everything's in house. I got the labels, I got the product ... *(Porker speaks up. He hasn't, of course, been to the bathroom. He has simply stepped out of sight.)*
PORKER. What product?
SALLY. We're gonna' rewrap everything we got. Tommy Fusco's brought me labels from Mass Coastal. We're in business here, yes?
ARLYNE. *You* did this, Salvatore?
SALLY. I did, yuh, I made the call myself ... I made the sale.
JOSIE. Does Markie know this?
SALLY. I told Markie I could move the stock, yes ...
FLORENCE. We're selling off all the stock we've got?
SALLY. I'm making work. I'm covering overhead ...
ARLYNE. Are we makin' a profit?
SALLY. What is this? I have to make reports to the wrappers? *(False laugh. After a pause, Sally continues; answers Arlyne.)* We're breakin' even. We're payin' ourselves. We're makin' our own work ...*(There is another small pause. Then Sally screams his orders,*

officiously.) I want everybody on unwrappin'. I want all the labels pulled and then we'll all go on to wrapping ... Could we please start? *(Everybody starts unwrapping boxes of frozen fish.)* Porker, go get the rest of the stock ... *(Nods to Porker.)* Let's go. *(Porker and Sally exit, with handtrucks, after leaving crates at end of wrapping table.)*

ARLYNE. I don't like the sound of this ...

JOSIE. It doesn't sound great ...

FLORENCE. Looks like the end of the road.

RUTHIE. How so, Floey?

FLORENCE. You can't sell fish if you got no fish to sell!

MAUREEN. Sally must know what he's doing ...

FLORENCE. How come you say *that*, Maureen?

MAUREEN. I dunno'.

MARLENA. He's good looking ...

FLORENCE. Right. You got it ... *(Smiles, nods to Maureen.)* Your cousin catches on fast.

MARLENA. Something wrong?

FLORENCE. Nope. *(Porker re-enters with handtruck loaded with cartons of frozen product.)*

PORKER. This don't look good ...

RUTHIE. It's work, like Sally said ...

PORKER. If we sell off all our stock, under-priced, then we ain't got nothin' ta' play with ... to broker. I mean, where's the future? *(Florence laughs. Sally re-enters, unloads his truckload of frozen product.)*

SALLY. If ya's all are smart, you'll work hard now, and save yo'rselves a job for tomorrow ... if you get my message. *(Sally exits again. The women unwrap product, diligently.)*

ARLYNE. No harm in workin' hard ...

JOSIE. When have we ever done anything but?

MARLENA. Hard work's the best thing in the world, really ...

MAUREEN. The Japanese give their first loyalty to their work, second to their families. That's why their country's making so much money ...

FLORENCE. Same thing here, ain't it? Who do you know who's

givin' their first loyalty to their family? *(Florence moves U. to breading machine. After a moment's work, Arlyne sings, alone, not conscious of anyone listening, or caring.)*
ARLYNE. "If you want a dooo-right-all-night's womannnn..." *(Thinks; speaks.)* If John Wayne had been a singer, he would have sounded just like Willie Nelson ...
JOSIE. I think that's true ...
FLORENCE. After Willie Nelson's dead, he'll sound just like John Wayne.
PORKER. I don't get it.
FLORENCE. *(Explains.)* John Wayne's dead now. After Willie Nelson's dead, they'll sound alike. Get it?
PORKER. *(Disgusted.)* What's *with* you?
RUTHIE. *(To Marlena.)* My mother's hung up on John Wayne ...
ARLYNE. I'm not "hung up". I *like* John Wayne. I enjoyed his acting. He was excellent!
JOSIE. They say he had a tiny organ. Miniscule.
PORKER. I'm in the room, ya' know.
JOSIE. So what?
PORKER. I hear what you're sayin'.
JOSIE. "Miniscule" isn't dirty, Porker. It means the same as "tiny" ...
MAUREEN. ... like your Toyota ...
RUTHIE. ... like your Christmas bonus ...
FLORENCE. ... like your *mind* ...
JOSIE. ... like John Wayne's wee-wee!
PORKER. What is *with* this one?
RUTHIE. John Wayne's real name was Marion Morrison ...
ARLYNE. She does this to annoy me.
RUTHIE. It was *so!*
FLORENCE. Marion?
RUTHIE. It's in my "What To Name The Baby" book. Marion Something Morrison. They have this whole long list of famous name-changes.
PORKER. John Wayne was a fag?

FLORENCE. What's this?
PORKER. Isn't that what Ruthie just said? John Wayne had a girl's name ... *(Sally re-enters with another handtruck load.)*
SALLY. Now, what's the chatter?
PORKER. John Wayne was a fag!
SALLY. What's this?
PORKER. Ruthie found it in a book. He was a fag. He had a girl's name.
SALLY. What are you saying, Martino?
PORKER. John Wayne's real name was a goddam *girl's name* ... The Duke, huh? The *Duchess*, that's what!
SALLY. If you ain't the fuckin' limit! *(Sally dumps the contents of his handtruck and exits, angrily.)*
PORKER. What's with Sally? Everything I say pisses him off.
FLORENCE. Maybe 'cause Sally's a girl's name, huh?
PORKER. What the hell are you *tellin'* me here? You *know* somethin'? What's with this insinuendo, huh? *(The women roar with laughter. Shimma walks down staircase, from kitchen, above. End of laugher.)*
SHIMMA. I called into Boston. I can't allow the rewraps to go out of here. I don't care if you've been doin' it before. I can't allow it to go out of here, now. *(Pauses.)* It's not my decision ...
PORKER. What are you saying here?
SHIMMA. Once product is wrapped, it's wrapped and it's gotta' be shipped.
PORKER. But, we didn't wrap it! It's bought already wrapped. It's our stock. That which we don't process and pack ourselves we buy, already wrapped. It's our stock. That's the business ... Oh, shit! *(Porker runs off-stage, to get Sally. There is a pause.)*
SHIMMA. It's not my decision ...
FLORENCE. So, if you get this plant closed down, then what?
SHIMMA. I'm not lookin' to get this plant closed down. I'm just doing my job. If I don't, somebody else will come in and do the very same thing ... *(Shrugs.)* I'm not lookin' to get any plant closed down ... *(Sally enters on the run; skids to a stop.)*

SALLY. What's this?

SHIMMA. I can't approve the rewraps. There's no way.

SALLY. There's nothin' you can do about it. There's a government pass on every package ... It all passed.

SHIMMA. Not after you unwrap the package there isn't ...

SALLY. The government doesn't pass the label. It's the *product* that's been passed ...

SHIMMA. You've never heard of "shelf-life"? This stuff's double-dated ...

SALLY. What shelf-life? These are frozen goods! What the hell are you talking about?

SHIMMA. It's not my decision. I called Boston ... I gotta red-tag.

SALLY. Now, wait a minute. Wait a fucking minute, here ... You ain't gonna' red-tag none of this product ... *(Sally starts to move in toward Shimma.)*

PORKER. Hey, Sally, come on ...

SALLY. You ain't closin' us down, sist'ah!

SHIMMA. I'm only doing my job! *(Sally arrives at Shimma, grabs her, backs her against wall. He raises his fist.)*

FLORENCE. *Don't, Sal!*

PORKER. *Sal! (Sally is about to hit Shimma, when, suddenly, Ruthie screams out.)*

RUTHIE. *Oh, God, Mama, it's coming! The baby! Oh, God! (Everybody turns and looks.) Oh, God, Mama, it's coming NOW! It's coming FAST! (There is a moment's pause.)*

BLACKOUT.

END OF SCENE ONE.

Scene Two

Fade in music: Otis Redding sings on tape: "Oh, she may be weary... Young girls do get weary... wearing that same shaggy dress... but, when she gets weary... try a little tenderness..."*
Music fades out.

Lights up in plant, fifteen minutes later. Maureen, Florence and Marlena are sitting, center, smoking cigarettes. N.B. The 1st glow from their cigarettes is the cue for the stage-lighting. Ruthie and Arlyne are off-stage, in the lounge. Ruthie is about to deliver her baby. Josie and Sally are with them. Shimma is in her kitchen, on the telephone. Porker enters from off-stage.

FLORENCE. How's she doin'?
PORKER. Any second now ... Any word from the doctor?
FLORENCE. She's callin' his office. He should'a been here by now ...
PORKER. He can't be here if he doesn't know about it ...
MARLENA. I was born on my father's boat ... *(Pauses.)* My mother was overdue, so my father took her out for a ride on the boat, to shake her up ... It worked ... Of course, I was a third baby for my mother. *(Pauses.)* I guess I came too fast ...
PORKER. You *what* too fast?
FLORENCE. Jesus, Porker, you are *disgusting! (To Marlena.)* One thing on his mind! Honest ta' God!
PORKER. What's with you? I was just interested in what she was sayin' ...

*See special note on copyright page.

FLORENCE. Oh, yuh, sure ...
PORKER. *(To Marlena.)* I was born on my father's lobster boat. Same thing, kinda'. My mother was frightened she'd have me while my father was out on the boat ... So, she came along ... I was her fourth baby. *(Smiles.)* They say they figured if she went into labor, they'd have time to get up to Addison-Gilbert, 'counta' they weren't too far out, just lobsterin' off of Bass Rocks ... *(Shrugs.)* I guess they figured it wrong ...
FLORENCE. A long line of great thinkers ...
MAUREEN. My Uncle Kevin got born in the old Central Grammar School. My grandmother used to clean there. Then he went to school there himself ...
FLORENCE. Didn't he teach there, too?
MAUREEN. That's my point. After he finished college up to Salem Teachers, he taught there ... all his life 'til they retired him at sixty-five ... Now, it's city-subsidized housing and he's movin' in there. Imagine: born in the same buildin', school in the same buildin' ... and now he'll be livin' there!
FLORENCE. The Central Grammar School?
MAUREEN. Practically the same room he taught in ... Same floor. It's amazing, huh?
FLORENCE. I got two aunts livin' up there. Nice place ...
MAUREEN. A whole life, in one building ...
FLORENCE. Arlyne's like that with this place. She started here, same as my Mum, when she was about fifteen. She must be, what?, sixty, now?
MAUREEN. Close to it ... she's been shop stewardess here, probably thirty-five years ...
FLORENCE. That's why my Mum was so happy ta' get laid off. It was like a ticket *out'ta* this place ... *(Pauses; then bitterly.)* Bloodless fuckin' people, layin' her off after so many years, huh?
PORKER. Puts the food on the table ...
FLORENCE. What the hell are you *sayin'*, Porker?
PORKER. I'm just sayin' that workin' here puts food on the table. That's not too complex an idea, is it? What's with your attitude? *(We hear: Siren, off-stage, to indicate arrival of police car. We might*

also see the glow of a flashing red light reflected on a wall. Shimma enters from kitchen, then goes off-stage to back room, to Ruthie, and C. Josie pokes her head in from back room, calls to Florence and Porker.)

JOSIE. He's here. *(Josie disappears back into back room. there is a moment's pause. The sound of the siren stops. The car has arrived. Arlyne appears, poking head into room, then re-exits, into back room. There is another moment's pause. Sally appears from back room, for a brief statement.)*

SALLY. The doctor's here! *(Nervous laugh.)* I sent him around back to the loading door. *(Sally re-exits into back room.)*

FLORENCE. Gives me the creeps, havin' the police come here like that again ... so soon ...

MAUREEN. Me, too ...

FLORENCE. Seein' the son-of-a-bitch comin' in, same look on his face ... *(She imitates Sally.)* The doctor's here ... *(Adds in Sally's nervous laugh. Florence punches her fist into her hand.)* Gives me total willies, that's what. Saddest thing there is. Saddest goddam thing there is, I swear to God! *(Florence turns away. Maureen explains to Marlena.)*

MAUREEN. When Dot died — She's the one we was tellin' ya' about — the doctor showed up in the Gloucester police cruiser, same way.

MARLENA. She died *here?*

MAUREEN. We found her in the freezer, when we opened up.

PORKER. *I* found her.

MARLENA. Oh, Jees. That must'a be'n *weird!*

MAUREEN. Same exact sound: police cruiser with the siren goin' soft-like, then the brakes screechin', stoppin' ...

FLORENCE. Mist'ah Macho comin' in with that same look on his face: half puppy-dog, half shit-eating grin ... *(Imitates Sally again, words and laugh.)* "The doctor's here ..." *(Pauses.)* Saddest goddam thing there is ...

PORKER. *(Softly.)* Floey? Hey, Floey, c'mon, huh ... *(Florence looks at Porker, half smiles, bravely. The two old friends share a private moment of grief.)*

MARLENA. *(After a pause.)* What ... happened?

PORKER. I opened up, same as usual ... hit the daytime generators, mopped up, set out the waste cartons, the usual. Then I went into the freezer to load a pallet with blocks. We were doin' Grade "A" orders for McDonald's then ... before we lost the account ... The freezer was full of exhaust fumes ... *(Without pause.)* Dotty was on her back on top of a stack of #6 blocks. She was wearin' her dress, street shoes, lab coat on top, open ...

MAUREEN. She killed herself ...

MARLENA. No kidding?

MAUREEN. Length of garden-hose tapped into the freezer-engine ...

PORKER. The fumes were wicked ... *(Pauses.)* To tell you the God's honest truth, I still didn't think she was dead. Her eyes were open and she was starin' straight at me ...

MARLENA. That musta' be'n creepy!

PORKER. She was kinda half-smilin' ... her eyes all sad ...

MAUREEN. The doctor caught a ride up in the police cruiser. They were all in Dunkin' Donuts when the call came in ...

PORKER. Co-incidence ...

MAUREEN. Same exact sound: police cruiser with the sireen goin', soft-like, then the brakes screechin', stoppin' ...

PORKER. She was in the family way. The G.D. Times said she was "despondent" ...

MAUREEN. She was havin' Sal's baby ...

FLORENCE. No, she wasn't. She killed it, two days before, over Beverly. She went to Sal and he told her to kill it ... set it up for her ...

MAUREEN. Dot's a super devout Catholic, too. Her whole family. Her brother's a priest, down Revere ...

FLORENCE. It drove her nuts, killin' off the baby ...

PORKER. Made her despondent ...

FLORENCE. Sal made her kill it ... *(Sally enters, looks about, smiles.)*

SALLY. Any second now ... *(Laughs.)* Too much for meee ... *(Smiles.)* It's an amazing thing. Absolutely amazing ...

JOSIE. *(Pokes her head into room; excitedly.)* It's the baby! The head's come out!
PORKER. Boy or girl?
JOSIE. Just a *head's* out! Jesus, Porker! *(Josie exits again into back room. Sally looks up at Florence, not smiling.)*
FLORENCE. Are you gonna' shoot this one with a gun? Or are you gonna' let this one live?
SALLY. *(Shows his palms to Florence.)* Right. Great. Fine.
PORKER. What's this?
FLORENCE. You're quite a fella', Sal ...
SALLY. That's what they tell me.
FLORENCE. I hope you die.
PORKER. Hey, Floey, what gives here?
SALLY. I probably will ... fifty-sixty-seventy years after you do, I hope ...
PORKER. Hey, Sally, what gives? *(We hear: The sound of a baby crying, softly, off-stage. Maureen crosses herself, as does Marlena and Sally.)* Goddd ... *(Josie runs in.)*
JOSIE. It's a girl! *(Everyone cheers enthusiastically. Josie runs off, returning to Ruthie, off-stage.)*
MARLENA. I love girls.
SHIMMA. *(Enters, smiling.)* It's a girl! *(Shimma goes up stairs, to her kitchen; closes door. Arlyne enters, smiling.)*
ARLYNE. Girl! *(Everyone cheers, again. They gather around Arlyne, hugging and kissing her: children around a triumphant mother.)*
MAUREEN. How's Ruthie?
ARLYNE. Hardly a peep. We deliver easy. *(She looks around at Porker and the others, smiling at them, happily.)* Wonderful thing, isn't it, bein' born right here, right in the middle of it ... *Gawdd!* *(Sobs.)* I wish my mother coulda' been alive ta' see it. Gawdd! *(Smiles, instant recomposure.)* It's a girl! Ruthie's fine. You wanna' come see?
MAUREEN. Great! *(To Marlena.)* Wanna'?
MARLENA. Great! *(Maureen and Marlena exit into back room. Josie re-enters, momentarily.)*
JOSIE. *(To Arlyne.)* She's askin' for ya' ... *(Josie and Arlyne re-exit.*

Sally, Porker and Florence are alone on stage. Sally nods to Porker.)
SALLY. Give us two minutes to ourselves here, okay?
PORKER. I'm not listening. *(Showing his palms.)* I'm not listening! *(Sally goes to Florence.)*
SALLY. Can I try to explain something here? *(Florence looks at Sal, wordlessly; shrugs.)* I was seventeen, Carmella was sixteen. All'a fuckin' *Gloucester* knew what was happening! I mean, come onnn ... two kids leave high school and get married 'cause they're *so in love?* Seventeen years old, standing up in Our Lady Of The Good Voyage Church, looking out the door to Destino's while Father Gambriana's sayin' "Do you, Salvatore, take this woman ...?" And you know what I'm really doin'? I'm lookin' out the door across the street and I'm seein' Porker's girlfriend, Jumbo-jet Josie Evangelista, hoppin' up the steps to Destino's for her second cold-cut sub of that particular morning, and I'm thinkin' about what it would be like to be bouncing up and down on her moons-over-Miami! *(Porker quickly runs to top of stairs to basement/changing room; checks to be certain that Josie can't hear.)*
PORKER. Josie's nothin *like* my girlfriend!
SALLY. Yuh. Sure. And you're not in love with Florence here, neither, right?
PORKER. What's this?
SALLY. I thought you wasn't listening!
PORKER. I'm not!
FLORENCE. Did you?
SALLY. Did I what?
FLORENCE. Bounce on Josie?
SALLY. I did ... about two weeks after the wedding. *(Pauses, looks away: a private moment.)* I'm seventeen and Carmella's *six*teen, and nobody's got the sense ta' get it taken care of! I mean, come *onnn.* Carmella was probably second or third best grades in the whole junior class ... already accepted down to Salem Teacher's, right? Futures? Forget about it! "The family *Pride*", my father's tellin' me. Her old man ... you remember looney Yo-Yo Shimmataro, before he fell out of his brother's dragger?

PORKER. I remember Yo-Yo ... No great brain *there* ...
SALLY. Yuh, well, Yo-Yo corners me, over back of the old Rockaway. I was drinkin' beers all night with Bootsy McMahon, and I'm off havin' myself a piss ... my thing is out, and all's'a sudden there's Carmella's old man right beside my doo-dad. I'm thinkin' "Swell! He's gonna' cut it off!" and I hear Yo-Yo sayin' in this sincere fuckin' voice: "I've knocked her mother up, same way, and we've been together thirty-something years, already, and we're *pretty happy*, sometimes. I'm glad Carmella's marrying a *man*!" What'd he think Carmella was marrying: a fucking *toad*? *(Pause.)* Seventeen years old: they fix us up with a two-day honeymoon in some summah cottage Carmella's mother cleans, over Riverdale. She's got the key so we use it for two days ... the place stinks of mold and mustiness. Then we both start workin' here, at North Shore Fish: Carmella stays on the line, wrappin', til she's big like Ruthie ... Me: I start right out in the office, coverin' Markie Santuro's ass, which I will never stop doin' til I fucking *die!* And Carmella goes home to mind the baby. She closes the door behind her and she never gets to see daylight again! *(Confidentially, to Florence, trying to exclude Porker.)* Let me ask you a question, Florence, straight and simple: Knowin' how I wrecked Carmella's life as I did ... not to mention knowin' how I've probably been the worst husb'in in the history of the whole North Shore, tell me something: How m'I s'pose'ta walk out on this person, Florence? How?
PORKER. Walk out on who, Sal? Walk out on who? *(To Florence.)* What's he sayin', huh? What's he talkin' about? Come on, you guys? What gives? *(Josie re-enters, she is upset, holding back tears. She makes eye contact with Florence and Sally; smiles, bravely.)*
JOSIE. Nice little girl ... *(Then, without warning, Josie goes directly to Porker and folds herself into his arms, weeping.)* Makes me so sad ... *(Sobs.)* Oh, God, it makes me so sad ...
PORKER. What does, Jose?
JOSIE. Babies bein' born ... *(Sobs.)* If I weren't so fat, he'd come home, wouldn't he?
PORKER. You're not fat! *(To Florence and Sally.)* Is she fat? *(Florence shrugs. Sally shrugs. Porker makes a fist at both of them. He*

grabs a coffee mug, fills it from Maureen's thermos; hands mug to Josie.) Drink some of my sister Rose's coffee. It'll make your troubles seem miniscule. *(She takes mug; sits on steps. She tries not to cry. She sips the coffee. She makes a face. Porker sits beside Josie on steps.)* I think she adds Oregano. *(Josie smiles; briefly. And then she speaks, sadly.)*

JOSIE. He used to touch me all the time. I don't just mean high school: I mean years and years afta' ... *(Sobs.)* I don't know why I eat so much, Porker. I get so *frustrated* ... doin' the same things day in and day out ... havin' no money ... seein' the same bunch'a'ya's, day in, day out ... sayin' the same dumb things ... *(Sobs.)* Don't take this personal. It's not personal. It's not against any of ya's, honest ta' God, but, I really hate my life ... *(Pauses.)* I'm sick of the neglect. Being his wife is like being a dog in a dead man's house. *(Josie is now a sobbing jelly-mass in Porker's arms. Porker looks around helplessly at Florence. Florence starts to cry. She holds her stomach and she wails with grief. Sally goes to her; speaks softly.)*

SALLY. Floey?

FLORENCE. What?

SALLY. I'm tryin' to say something to you, Florence. Something about *life* I think I'm finally learnin' ... something that's, I dunno', *appropriate* right now about, well, *us.*

FLORENCE. Yuh, swell, let's hear it.

SALLY. People like us are like pieces of wood floating on the water. We float in — sometimes we touch — sometimes, we even *bang together* ... but, then, we float off. We're not really in control of these things, Florence. There's like some *big tide* moving us here and there ... We can't really be *blamed.* *(Florence hits Sally. It is a startling backhand blow.)*

JOSIE. Hey! Florence!

PORKER. Ah, shit, you guys, c'mon, will ya's ... *(Sally holds his hand to his cheek.)*

FLORENCE. Tell Carmella to set a couple of extra places at the table for next Christmas dinner. Tell Carmella I'll be comin' over for next Christmas ... me and the baby.

SALLY. I'm s'pose'ta walk out on her 'cause you and I are *so much*

in love, right? What a joke, huh? I oughta' send it in to CBS-TV. They can use it on the television! *(He starts away from Florence; stops; turns to her again.)* You wanna' tell Carmella and Little Sal and Michael and Angela about everything, this is fine with me, you do that! You do that ... and a' course, then I get to tell Bradley and Emily about their mother bein' the Town Pump, right? *Florence points her finger at Sally and seems to want to yell something accusatory, but, cannot form the words. She sobs, instead, pointing her finger inscrutably. Sally moves towards Florence, just as Maureen and Marlena re-enter. They are both smiling brightly.)*
MAUREEN. She's beautiful ...
MARLENA. She's *sooo* nice!
MAUREEN. You should go in and see her, Josie. It'll make you feel good.
MARLENA. She's really such a nice little baby ... *(Maureen and Marlena feel the pain in the air.)*
SALLY. I'm gonna go tell Markie. I gotta' tell him about the baby and about the red-taggin'. I gotta report in to Markie. *(Sally turns on his heel and exits, into back office.)*
JOSIE. It's all big loud thunder and very little rain. You know what I mean? *(Sighs.)* Cookie's giving me about half what he used'ta' ... and that's with me hounding him day and night. My fatha' keeps tellin' me to take nothin' ... to let him pick up the bills and just throw Cookie out altogether ... *(Pauses; weeps.)* I'm thirty years old. I don't want my fatha' payin' my bills ... *(Sobs.)* My fatha' wants to kill him, ya' know. My fatha' knows that Cookie's be'n beating me. *(Sobs.)* Before you beat a dog, you better make sure whose dog it is. That's the way I see it.
FLORENCE. A dog is a dog. [is a dog]. That's the way *I* see it.
JOSIE. I don't like that mouth of yours, sistah! You got something shitty between you and Salvatore, this is fine, this is great, but this is between the rotten two of ya's, so, don't be draggin' us all inta the middle! Nobody's got the guts ta' bring it up, but we all remember the price certain people paid for gettin' caught between the pair of ya's sluggin' it out, okay?

PORKER. Maybe you oughta just leave it be, Josie, huh?
FLORENCE. What are you gettin' at?
PORKER. Me?
FLORENCE. Her!
JOSIE. What I'm sayin' here is maybe if you never started in with Sal, things might'a' be'n a little different for Dot, huh? You ever think of that?
PORKER. Hey, Josie, Jesus! Is *that* what you were sayin'?
FLORENCE. Yo'r mouth is as big as your ass, ain't it?
PORKER. Hey, come *on*, will ya's!
FLORENCE. *(Circling towards Josie.)* I seen Cookie down the Rigger, ya' know ...
JOSIE. Yuh, so?
FLORENCE. So, am I sayin' things out loud?
JOSIE. What am I sayin' out loud?
FLORENCE. What are you? *Simple?* Your ears can't hear what your mouth is speakin'?
JOSIE. I didn't say nothin'! Did I say anything bad, Porker? You're right here. You heard! Did I?
PORKER. What do I know? People say things. It's intense around here right now. No big deal ...
FLORENCE. Not to you, maybe, shit-for-brains, but, if I'm carryin', that's my personal stuff and havin' it talked about in front of everybody is no little deal to *meee!*
JOSIE. Who the hell said you was carrying?
PORKER. Now, you lost me there, Flo ... I gotta' tell you: You lost me there ...
JOSIE. *(To Porker.)* Did you hear me say she was carrying?
PORKER. Carrying what?
JOSIE. A baby, you dodo!
PORKER. A baby? You're having a baby, Florence?
FLORENCE. Come off the shit, Porker! Sal told you. He wouldn't keep something like that to himself ...
PORKER. Cross my heart!
FLORENCE. *Porker!*
PORKER. Okay, so he said something, but, honest'-ta'- God, I

didn't believe him for a second. Sal's always braggin' about this and that, right? ... How far along are you?
JOSIE. Jesus, Porker, what's *with* you?
FLORENCE. I'm havin' it taken care of during lunch-break, tomorrow. I made the appointment ... over Beverly. That's where lady-killer sends his ladies, right?
JOSIE. Don't let Arlyne hear ...
FLORENCE. What do I care? You think the Pope's gonna' be any happier if there's one more pathetic kid runnin' around Gloucester, wonderin' where the hell his fatha' is ... wonderin' why the hell he was put on Earth? For *this*? For cutting and packin' TV-fucking-dinners? Taste-O-The-fucking-Sea-Fish-Fingers??? What are you all? *Crazy???*
JOSIE. You know what Arlyne will say to that: "We're in the fish business. We're fish people. We're doin' what we were born to do ...
FLORENCE. Can you believe this one? This is not the fish business, Josephine! This is the non-union, bottom-of-the-barrel, end-of-the-road, frozen, breaded *dung* business! I know what fish is. Fish is alive until you kill it. Fish is something that bleeds when you cut it open. You see this already-wrapped-and-unwrapped-twenty-seven-times-frozen-*dung*? *(She breaks apart a frozen fish-brick into its component parts.)* One little fish-neck, two little fish-backs, piece of a tail, piece of another tail ... Answer me a question: Did you ever in your entire life see anybody actually *eat this shit*? *(Sally walks out of the back office; re-enters; stands facing Porker, Florence, Maureen and Marlena. He is ashen; whitefaced.)*
PORKER. Sally.
FLORENCE. *What?*
PORKER. Sally's back ...
FLORENCE. So what?
SALLY. I think one of you should stop me ...
PORKER. What?
SALLY. Me: I should be stopped.
PORKER. From what, Sal?
SALLY. You'll see "from what?" when I get to her goddam door

...*(Sally climbs stairs to kitchen. He screams at Shimma.)* Get out here, you Commie KGB pig! *(Shimma presses her nose against the window, frightened. She locks door. Satisfied that door is locked, Sally goes to door, bangs on same.)* GET... OUT HERE !!! GET *(Bang.)* OUT *(Bang.)* HERE *(Bang, bang, bang.)* !!! *(Shimma stares out from behind the glass, trapped, but safe from Sally's rage. Sally kicks the door, three sharp kicks. He then climbs on structure, screaming in through window at a terrified Shimma.)*

PORKER. Hey, Sally, what's *with* you?

SALLY. You better stop me, Martino, or else I'm gonna' break this door down and murder this one ...

PORKER. Why now? What's she done now? She couldn't have red-tagged nothin' more 'cause we haven't mastered nothin' more. Nothin's gone into the master pack for more'n an hour and a half.

SALLY. Markie's sold the plant.

PORKER. What?

SALLY. You have waxey ears or what? Markie's sold the goddam plant out from under us ...

FLORENCE. What are you sayin', you?

SALLY. Am I not speaking the King's fucking English? Markie Santuro has sold the plant. North Shore Fish is sold.

FLORENCE. To who?

JOSIE. To who?

MAUREEN. To whom?

MARLENA. What's happening?

MAUREEN. He's saying the plant's been sold ...

MARLENA. Will you still get your paid vacation?

MAUREEN. Jesus, Marlena, I'm just hearin' this same as you ...

MARLENA. I don't wanna' be a pain in the ass, but, I've got to schedule out my time ...

MAUREEN. Shut up! *(Maureen moves to Sally.)* Who'd Markie sell the plant to, Sal? *(Sally doesn't answer.)* Sal?

SALLY. It's gonna be a fitness center ...

FLORENCE. What?

SALLY. Nautilus, aerobics classes, that shit ...
JOSIE. I'll join up! My prayers are answered!
PORKER. Are you shittin' me, Morella? This plant is *sold?*
SALLY. Sold. The equipment goes on the dump. The new people move in as soon as possible ...
PORKER. Like when?
SALLY. I dunno' ... Tuesday, Wednesday ... We hav'ta' clear our personal stuff out'ta here, today ...
PORKER. Wait a minute, wait a minute. North Shore Fish is sold and it's gonna' have weight-lifting and dancing classes startin' *Tuesday* or *Wednesday? (Laughs.)* This is a fact of life?
SALLY. *(Smiling.)* This is a definite fact of life. There is no changing this. Markie's had these fitness people on "hold" for about six weeks, 'til he saw whether or not the business turned around. He's pretty torn up about it, himself, I can tell you that. This plant's been in the Santuro family more'n a hundred years ...
PORKER. *(Laughing and snorting.)* Wait a minute, wait a minute, wait a minute! This plant is definitely sold and weight-lifting and Nautilus are definitely comin' in here as soon as possible, maybe Tuesday or Wednesday of this coming *week?*
SALLY. *(Starts laughing, infected by Porker's laugh.)* Definite, definite, definite ... *(Florence and the others giggle as well, also infected by Porker's laugh.)*
PORKER. You're not my boss, anymore, Morella? You're not over me? I'm not under you? This here set-up between us is over and done?
SALLY. *(Laughing.)* Over and done. *(Without warning, with total purpose and precision, Porker goes to Sally and punches him in the stomach.)*
PORKER. You miserable prick! You greaseball, fuck-your-own-children, miserable brown-nose prick! *(Porker pummels Sally with slaps, swats and punches. This is the fight that Porker has stored away for some twenty years: since 5th grade. The fight is, thus, like that: formless; childlike ... a school-yard brawl.)*
MAUREEN, FLORENCE & MARLENA. —Hey, Porker, off him ...

—Hey, Porker, stop ...
—Grab his arms ...
—Porker, knock it off ...
—He's killin' Sal!
—Stop it, Alfred!
—Stop punching, Porker!
—You split his lip!
—Porker, you'll kill him! *(Instant chaos: Porker and Sally are in a heap. The women pile on and try to pull Porker off of Sally.)*
PORKER. *(A tad hysterical.)* I'LL KILL HIM! I'LL RIP HIS HEART OUT! I'LL BREAK HIS ARMS OFF! GIMME HIS MISERABLE TONGUE AND LEMME PULL IT OUT'TA HIS MISERABLE MOUTH! LEMME KILL HIM! I WAITED MY WHOLE FUCKIN' LIFE FOR THIS! GIVE HIM TO MEEEE!
FLORENCE. *(Sees Ruthie coming up stairs, from below.)* The baby! Stop! The baby! *(Ruthie enters, supported by Arlyne. Ruthie's hair is matted, stringy. She is sweatly, exhausted, but joyously aglow. She wears Shimma's white lab-coat; carries her baby, swaddled in white towels. [N.B. A note on the "baby": not a baby-doll, but, instead, a couple of towels swaddled in a couple of towels.] Porker stops his rant when he sees Ruthie. All others look up as well, amazed. The women pull Porker off of Sally, who rises from the floor, slowly. His lip is split, bloodied. Sally holds his jaw; Ruthie holds her baby. A unique class-reunion photo could be shot now.)*
RUTHIE. I'm totally fine. Don't any of you worry. They're takin' me up Addison-Gilbert, but, it's only for the rules. I could go straight home if I had to. I'm totally fine ...
ARLYNE. I'm gonna' run up to the hospital with Ruthie while they check her and the baby out ... if that's okay with you, Sal ...
FLORENCE. *(To Sally; sternly.)* Don't you tell her!
SALLY. It's fine, Arlyne, fine. No problem. Have a good weekend.
ARLYNE. What happened, Sal?
SALLY. Why? What's the matter?

ARLYNE. Your lip's all bloody.
SALLY. I fell down.
ARLYNE. The doctor's still out in the cruiser, if you hustle out there ...
FLORENCE. He's okay.
MAUREEN. He's fine, Arlyne. It's superficial.
ARLYNE. It's on your coat, too. It looks like you've been cleaning live fish.
FLORENCE. Dead fish.
ARLYNE. Hmmm?
FLORENCE. He's fine, Arlyne. Go with Ruthie ...
RUTHIE. I'm naming her "Roxanne" ... *(There is a embarrassed pause: un ange qui passe.)*
FLORENCE. Don't do that, Ruthie. "Roxanne" is a shitty name ...
RUTHIE. You think so?
FLORENCE. It's *horrible.* She'll hate being "Roxanne" ...
RUTHIE. You all think so?
MAUREEN. I don't like it... 　　　PORKER. I wouldn't..
JOSIE. It sounds kinda' *cheap,* don't'cha think?... 　SALLY. I wouldn't, Ruthie. Roxanne's not really too great.
RUTHIE. *(To Marlena.)* How about you? I know you're temporary, but, I'm kinda' interested...
MARLENA. I dunno' ... Roxanne's okay, I guess ...
ARLYNE. I thought "Roxanne" was elegant.
FLORENCE. It's shitty, Ruthie. Trust me.
RUTHIE. How about "Florinda"?
FLORENCE. *(Rolls her eyes to heaven.)* Jesus, Ruthie!
RUTHIE. Well, how about "Joyce"?
FLORENCE. Yuh, well, maybe ...
JOSIE. Maybe ...
PORKER. Nothin' wrong with "Joyce"!
FLORENCE. I would go with "Joyce", Ruthie.
RUTHIE. Maybe I'll wait and go through the what-to-name-the-baby-book, again, tonight ... *(To the baby.)* You don't mind not

havin' a name one more day, huh? *(To all, with a giggle.)* She's cute, isn't she?
FLORENCE. I haven't seen her ... *(Walks to baby; looks.)* She's beautiful, Ruthie. She looks just like ... you and your mother. Same eyes.
RUTHIE. Yuh ... *(Ruthie crosses slowly, painfully, to the door; stops at threshold. To baby.)* Say "bye-bye" ...
ARLYNE. She'll be back ...
RUTHIE. No, she *won't*, Ma! *(Embarrassed by the suddenness of her response; to all.)* Just joshin' ... *(To Arlyne.)* I'm feeling just slightly weak. We'd better go ... *(To all.)* I'm really fine. Don't any of ya's worry.
MAUREEN. 'Bye, Ruthie. Congratulations ... congratulations to Earl, too!
MARLENA. Nice to meet'cha'.
RUTHIE. I'll probably be back in a week from Monday, Sal, if that's okay?
SALLY. Whatever you want, Ruthie, that's fine.
RUTHIE. *(Affectionately; admiringly.)* You're the greatest, Sal!

PORKER. *(Disgusted.)* Oh, yuh! "You're the greatest, Sal!"

SALLY. *(Touched.) Nawww!* Congratulations, Ruthie, huh? ... and say congratulations for me to Earl, too...

RUTHIE. I will. Come visit, everybody... *(Giggles.)* I guess you've seen the baby, already, but, come visit, anyhow...

FLORENCE. We will, Ruthie!

JOSIE. I'll come by, Sunday!

PORKER. 'Bye, Ruthie!

SALLY. 'Bye, Ruthie!

MARLENA. Nice to meet you both!

ARLYNE. Good weekend, everybody. Don't do anything I wouldn't do! *(Ruthie and Arlyne exit the play. There is a moment's pause. Suddenly, as though by some force of elision, Porker attacks Sally with precisely the same schoolboy intensity as before.)*
PORKER. Miserable prick! Lemme kill you! Lemme put you out'ta' yo'r misery! *(Once again, Porker muckles Sally and once again the women pile on top, pulling Porker from Sally before he does*

75

mortal damage.)
MAUREEN, FLORENCE & MARLENA. —Porker, come onnn ...
—Grab his arms ...
—You'll kill him ...
—He's a lunatic!
—Get off, Porker ...
—Stop hitting ... Porker ...
—Jesus, Porker, STOP!
PORKER. I'LL RIP HIS HEART OUT! I'LL TEAR HIS MISERABLE TONGUE OUT'TA HIS HEAD! *LET ME!!!* *(The two men are once again separated. Sally's lip is again cut and bleeding. Porker rages out of control, moaning and ranting. The three women try to hold him back.)*
FLORENCE. You gotta' calm down, Porker. You'll bust a blood vessel!
PORKER. Let me go, Florence! Let me at him!
FLORENCE. I can't do that, Pork!
PORKER. *(Breaks loose; charges at Sally, swatting him with terrycloth towel.)* You blew it, Morella! My grandfather worked in fish, my father worked in fish, and I am gonna work in fish. You can sink and submerge this plant but you can't pull real people like us down with you! I will bury you before I'll sink with you, and that is a fucking fact of life, you *faggot!*
SALLY. You split my lip, you *dick!*
PORKER. I'll split your dick, you *derr* ... you *peckerhead* ...you *pussy* ... *(Sally finds a wet rag, and swats back at Porker.)*
SALLY. I didn't put this plant under, you *dink* ... you *donk* ... you *diddlyshit.* I kept this plant goin'! I kept this plant alive! I breathed precious life inta' this operation. I put the food on your goddam table, Martino! *(To all.) All of ya's!* I kept you workin' ... kept you earnin' money. I put the food in your babies mouths, if you wanna' know the goddam truth of it! And this is the thanks I get!
FLORENCE. What are you? *Demented?*
SALLY. Yuh, right, I'm demented. Takes one to know one, Florence ...

PORKER. *(Screaming.)* Don't dignify the dork, Floey! Honest ta' Christ, just treat him like somethin' dead. Just treat him like a bad smell. Just act as though he ain't happenin', 'cause you *ain't*, Morella, you really *ain't!*

MAUREEN. *(Out of nowhere.)* Is my vacation paid, or what, Sal?

SALLY. What's that s'posed'ta' mean?

MAUREEN. What's that? Too *complex?* Is my vacation a paid vacation or a vacation that is not a paid vacation? Which?

SALLY. The plant is closin', Maureen. Closing. C-l-o-s...

MAUREEN. *(Picks up Josie's half-filled mug of Rose's old, cold coffee.)* Don't you fuckin' spell at me, you! *(Maureen pours coffee on Sally's head.)*

SALLY. Nice, thanks, Maureen, very nice ...

MAUREEN. You're lucky it wasn't boiling, 'cause that's what you deserve! You're lucky it wasn't a knife in your heart, 'cause that's what you *really* deserve! *(Maureen goes to Sally and spits at him.)* Scumbag! *(To Marlena.)* He's playin' up ta' all of us, all this time. He even comes on ta' old Arlyne, this one ...

SALLY. Come on, Maureen, huh?

MAUREEN. Sweet talkin' shit, keeping' all the girls scared they're gonna' get laid off if they don't come across ...

JOSIE. We all know the opposite to "laid off" workin' a line under you, don't we, Sally-boy?

SALLY. I never touched you once, Josephine, and you know it!

JOSIE. What are you? *Brain-damaged?*

SALLY. When? Name a single touch!

JOSIE. I'm s'posc'ta' spiel off when you touched me, in front of Floey and Reenie and Hotlips Martino?

SALLY. One touch: come on ... let's hear!

JOSIE. Greasy-Pole Contest, Stage Fort Park, under the old bandstand floor!

SALLY. That was years ago!

PORKER. What's this?

JOSIE. How'd you lose your memory? Horse step on your head?

PORKER. Is she makin' this up, or *what?*
SALLY. That was years and years ago!
JOSIE. Not so many...
SALLY. Eight!
JOSIE. Five!
SALLY. *(Shrugs.)* Five.
JOSIE. You were married to Carmella, already ... I was workin' under you, already ...
FLORENCE. Hard to find anybody who hasn't been workin' under this one ... if ya' catch my drift.
PORKER. What am I hearin' here?
FLORENCE. Kinda' hard ta' grasp, ain't it, Pork?
SALLY. I never thought I'd see the day you'd be blurtin' it out in front'a everybody...
JOSIE. Every dog has her day, Sal...
SALLY. You were goin' with Cookie, already, ya' know...
JOSIE. "Goin' with" is hardly "married to", you cheatin' bast'id!
PORKER. See? That's why I never did it...
FLORENCE. You never *did it,* Porker?!
PORKER. Ho, ho, that's rich. That's why I never got *married...*
JOSIE. What's why?
PORKER. On accounta' there's no point to it if nobody's ever gonna' be *faithful.*
FLORENCE. Also, on accounta' the fact that every goddam one of us said "no" when you asked us...
PORKER. *(After a beat.)* Now, that was a miserable cruel thing ta' say out loud.

MAUREEN. It was, Flo.	JOSIE. It was pretty low, Flo...	SALLY. It was, Flo.

FLORENCE. I guess...
MARLENA. *(After a pause.)* Is it true? Did he ask all'a ya's?
PORKER. Will you come on?
FLORENCE. All of us, all of Rockport, Manchester, Ipswich, Essex, even Woburn! *[Pronounced "woobin"]*

PORKER. Nice.
MARLENA. *(To Sally.)* Does this mean my workin' here next week is off, or what? Hey, I'm askin' you a question!
SALLY. What?
MARLENA. Does it?
SALLY. The plant is closed. Closed. What do you think it means? We clear out our stuff, we go home, we never come back unless we're takin' aerobics. Is that clear enough for you?
MARLENA. *(After a pause, to all: screams.)* He grabbed me in the freezer, you know...
SALLY in unison with PORKER. Come onnn...
MARLENA. Both of 'em! First him, then him! The greaseball pretty-boy jumped me and started pawin' all over! The little one snuck up and started in kissin' me. In the freezer!
FLORENCE. Teamed up?
MARLENA. Uh uh. One at a time. That one asked me to give him a hand with fish-fingers, then he jumped me on this huge frozen grey lump of something. I whacked my leg wick'id!
PORKER. When was this?
MARLENA. About 11, maybe 11:30, this morning ...
PORKER. *(Disgusted.)* Jesus, Sal ...
SALLY. What's with the "Jesus, Sal"? When did *he* come at you?
MARLENA. At least he said something nice! You just grabbed like I was, I dunno' ... *product!*
SALLY. I got no time for this. Come on, Martino. We got a freezer to inventory ...
PORKER. Do it yourself.
SALLY. What's this?
PORKER. Fuck you.
SALLY. This is exactly the gratitude I expect ...
PORKER. Fuck you and fuck your grandmother!
SALLY. This I won't be forgetting ... *(Sally makes a sign of the curse [Italian variety] at Porker; exits, swaggering, into the freezer. Porker is smiling.)*
FLORENCE. What'd he say?

MARLENA. Hmmm?

FLORENCE. This one: Porker: what "nice thing" did he say?

PORKER. What is the matter with you?

FLORENCE. Just curious, Pork ... *(She smiles at Marlena; pauses.)*

MARLENA. I don't remember ... *(Pauses.)* Something about me being "special" ...

FLORENCE. Special?

MARLENA. I dunno' ... *(Pauses.)* Something about me bein' "different from the hometown pigs" ...

JOSIE. Nice, Porker. Tasteful, too ...

FLORENCE. What? Like your bein' an out-a-town pig kinda' thing?

MAUREEN. Come on, you two!

MARLENA. I ought'a warn you that once I start swingin', I don't stop. I mean, I gotta *be* stopped. You follow my point?

FLORENCE. No, I can't follow your point. I got dropped on my head and I'm a stupid fool ... *(Talks to herself.)* Show her. How many fingers am I holding up? *(Holds up three fingers; answers her own question.)* Dahh, I dunno', Flo, *six? (To Marlena, menacingly.)* You wanna' swing, Suzie, you swing! If I ain't afraid of him or him, I certainly got no fuckin' fear of a bimbo like you!

PORKER. Hey, come onnn, will ya's, no rough stuff! *(Without warning, both Florence and Marlena slap Porker, at precisely the same time. Porker reels backwards, holding his face. He is totally humiliated. He confronts the women, Marlena first.)* I ain't gonna' hold you responsible for this, so, don't worry... *(To Florence.)* You neither ... *(To Maureen.)* Your bein' her cousin doesn't phase me against you, neither ... *(Nods in direction of freezer, where Sally exited.)* It's the asshole in the freezer I'm gonna' kill! *(Porker charges off into the freezer, screaming at Sally.)* Dukes up, Morella! You're gonna be dead meat! *(All pause. We hear: The sound of the freezer door slam shut* click closed. *Marlena looks at Florence.)*

MARLENA. I apologize for losing it. I was a little wiped out to hear the news that I was workin' for no money ...

FLORENCE. It's no sweat. I'm a little wiped out, myself.
(Shimma enters from office. She walks to Florence.)
SHIMMA. This wasn't my doing. I asked the owner straight out. He's had this offer on the table for two months, maybe more. This wasn't my doing ...
FLORENCE. What's the diff?
SHIMMA. I just wanted to say that ... I mean, this puts me out of work, too, you know ...
FLORENCE. No problem ...
SHIMMA. I've been waiting for this job to clear for me for weeks and weeks. I'm out now, too ...
FLORENCE. Nobody's pointing fingers. Don't sweat it ...
(Porker enters on the run, worried.)
PORKER. Sally's knocked out ...
JOSIE. Hey, good goin', Porker ...
PORKER. It wasn't my fault. He slipped ...
JOSIE. Don't be modest, Porker ...
PORKER. He hit his head and cut it ...
FLORENCE. What are you sayin'?
MAUREEN. Is he critical?
JOSIE. Is he dead?
PORKER. No, but he's hurt. He knocked himself out. We were rollin' around in the freezer and he whacked his head on this big chunk of tuna Markie keeps in there for personal use ... Maybe I should get the doctor back ...
MAUREEN. Is he still out cold?
PORKER. He came to, but he's groggy and his head's hurt bad ...
FLORENCE. Gushing?
PORKER. No, but cut ... and banged.
SHIMMA. Put some ice on it.
PORKER. You think so?
SHIMMA. I took First Aid in school ...
PORKER. Where'll I get ice?
FLORENCE. I thought you said you were in the freezer.
PORKER. Oh, yuh, right ...

FLORENCE. Jesus, Porker ... *(Porker exits off, again, on the run. There is a moment's pause. The women begin to pack their belongings, ready to leave.)*

SHIMMA. This is the first work I've had in four months ... At least I've got no stuff to pack up ...

FLORENCE. *(Emptying her locker.)* Makes no difference to me ... *(Pauses.)* I'm just about breaking even, anyhow ... *(Pauses.)* Babysitters make just about the same as me, after I pay tax and dues ... *(Pauses.)* My mother ain't gonna' live forever ... *(Pauses.)* Makes no difference to me ... Anybody got an extra shopping bag?

MAUREEN. *(Tosses bag to Florence.)* Here ...

FLORENCE. No sweat. I should chuck all'a this ...

MAUREEN. *(Packing.)* Me, too ... Anthony and I have been plannin' this trip for about two years now ... *(Pauses; smiles.)* He'll probably be happy to call it off now. I don't think he ever wanted to go, really ... he was just being nice ... He's got no real interest in seein' Connecticut ... just me.

FLORENCE. Connecticut? Is that where you were goin'? Connecticut?

MAUREEN. Connecticut has great natural beauty.

FLORENCE. You've never been to Connecticut?

MAUREEN. Yuh, well, so what?

FLORENCE. Don't miss Bridgeport. *Full* of natural beauty ...

MAUREEN. I'm not goin' anywhere. Anthony's gonna' be scared about makin' our mortgage payments, with me out'ta work again ...

JOSIE. At least you own a house ...

MAUREEN. Yuh, I guess ...

JOSIE. You could sell it. Arlyne said her cousin just sold her house over East Main Street for two-hundred-thousand ... They moved to Vermont — got a gorgeous place.

MAUREEN. I don't wanna' move to Vermont.

SHIMMA. We tried to buy something in town here ... Couldn't even come close ...

JOSIE. How come you wanted to buy here?
SHIMMA. My husband's from here ...
FLORENCE. From Gloucester?
SHIMMA. Yuh. Years back ...
JOSIE. What's his name?
SHIMMA. Billy Shimma ...
FLORENCE. He about thirty-eight?
SHIMMA. Thirty-seven ...
FLORENCE. There you go ...
JOSIE. Where'd he live?
FLORENCE. Lane's Cove, over by the sauna ...
SHIMMA. That's right.
JOSIE. *That* Billy Shimma? With the pink Buick?
SHIMMA. I never saw the Buick. I only heard about it ...
JOSIE. Small goddam world, huh? *(Porker leads Sally on. Sally holds a packette of frozen fish product against his head wound.)*
PORKER. I think he needs some stitches ...
JOSIE. Is he gushing?
PORKER. No, but it's open ... Somebody ought to run him up to the hospital ...
MARLENA. I'll do it. I've got a car ... *(Everybody looks at Marlena; surprised.)*
FLORENCE. The new girl.
MARLENA. I'm heading home anyhow. No point in paying a sitter for *this*. My kids are home from school already. No point in paying a sitter if the plant's closin' down ... *(Goes to Sally, looks at his head wound.)* I'll take you ... You know the way?
SALLY. I'm gonna' be okay ... *(To all.)* Don't any of ya's worry. I looked at my reflection in the chrome cover on the freezer pump and I've seen worse, so, don't any of ya's worry ... *(Pauses.)* Listen, I've got feelers out already and I've already gotten nibbles from a couple of places ... Maybe something's gonna's open up at Gorton's, for example. There's also something I don't wanna' mention, yet, but I want ya's all ta' know, definitely, when I'm settled, you're settled, and that is a promise ...
JOSIE. We know, Sal ...

SALLY. To tell you the God's honest truth, I'm glad Markie sold. He's been threatening for so long now ...
PORKER. Sally's be'n keepin' it from ya's ...
SALLY. I didn't want none of ya's ta' worry ... but I've seen this fitness clown hangin' around Markie for a couple'a weeks now ...
PORKER. The weightlifter type of musclebound Mafioso jamoca Earl kept seein' when he picked up our garbage. I kinda' suspected som'pin, myself, personally ...
SALLY. I kept it under my hat. I saw no point in every one of ya's bein' under the gun, to ...
PORKER. ... feelin' the pressure kind of thing ...
SALLY. To tell you the truth, I'm glad it's finally over. This way, I can set up something solid for all of us ...
JOSIE. We know you will, Sal ...
SALLY. You guys all ... mean something to me ...
JOSIE. You mean something to us, too, Sal ...
SALLY. I swear this to ya's all: I'll set up something new for all of us inside of three months, four at the very max ...
MAUREEN. We know you will, Sal. You've got my number, right?
SALLY. 'Course, I do. I got everybody's ...
FLORENCE. Yuh.
SALLY. *(Pauses; touches head.)* I'd better head up there ...
MARLENA. It was nice meeting you all ...
FLORENCE. Oh, yuh. It's gotta' have been one of the absolute high-points of my life ...
SHIMMA. I'm sorry it didn't work out. My husbin'll never believe this one, really ... *(Goes to Sally; offers hand.)* No hard feelin's, I hope ...
SALLY. Naw. I know you were just doin' a job ...
SHIMMA. Well ... *(Looks at all; shrugs.)* Good luck, everybody. I loved meeting ya's ... *(Exits.)*
JOSIE. Me, too ...
MAUREEN. Me, too ...
MARLENA. We'd better, huh?

SALLY. Yuh, sure ... *(Sally moves to Florence.)* I'm gonna' be sayin' "Goodbye", now ... *(Florence turns away from Sally. He starts to move to door; stops; turns again to face everyone. Suddenly, without warning, Sally begins to cry. He sobs and moans, openly, like a hurt child.)* It ain't fair, it ain't fuckin' fair! It ain't my fault. I did my job. I got out the product ... I got out the product! *(To all, embarrassed.)* It's the loss of blood, that's gettin' ta' me, probably. *(Pauses, clears his head; makes a pronouncement.)* I loved every woman who ever worked for me. I did. I'm not ashamed of it, neither. I'm a natural leader ... you watch me: before Labor Day. You watch me. I'll have ya's all workin' back under me in some local fish situation, before Easter. *(Exits.)*

MARLENA. 'By, everybody ... *(Exits. Maureen moves from her locker, carrying a huge stack of papers, books, stuff.)*

MAUREEN. I need a Sherpa ...

JOSIE. What's a Sherpa?

MAUREEN. They live in Nepal. They carry stuff up Mount Everest for explorers ...

FLORENCE. You know everything, don't you, Maureen?

MAUREEN. *(Blushes.)* I like to read about things ... *(Shrugs.)* Things interest me ... *(Drops some books.)* Shit! *(Picks them up.)* Lookit all this stuff. I never thought I'd be leavin' ' Got my own little Sawyer Free Library goin' ... *(Picks up to ost book; looks at it.)* A book on fish. I don't know anythin⟨ out fish, really ...

FLORENCE. Who knows anything about fish? I mean, fish don't tell you anything much, do they? You ask 'em a question, they flop around ... *(Ruefully, suddenly.)* What's the secret of life, Reenie?

MAUREEN. For fish, it goes like this. The female gets pregnant because she drops eggs and the male swims around and shoots his sperm at 'em ... at the eggs. The eggs pop open and about a million little fish swim around together. The females drop their eggs, the males shoot their sperm on 'em, and about ten million more fish pop out, swim around ...

FLORENCE. I'm sorry I asked ...

MAUREEN. The schools ... the fish that swim around together ...

they're all the same age. They never see their fathers again, after the sperm gets shot, never. They just swim around with fish their same age, and have their own little fish ... *(Smiles.)* Wanna' borrow the book?
FLORENCE. It sounds too depressing. I'll stick to Cosmopolitan.
MAUREEN. If Anthony and I bag Connecticut, maybe you and I can spend a morning down Salem? ... In the historic houses?
FLORENCE. Again?
MAUREEN. I was just thinkin' ...
FLORENCE. Sure. I'd like that, Reenie ... as long as we can skip the House of Seven Gables ... looks just like what I grew up in ... hit your head every time you move ... *(Maureen suddenly cries.)*
MAUREEN. I never thought we'd actually close up ...
PORKER. Don't cry, Reenie ...
MAUREEN. I better go ... *(Suddenly.)* Do you mind puttin' this stuff in the dumpster, Porker? There's nothin' here I need ...
PORKER. No problem ... You sure?
MAUREEN. I'll call you guys. 'Bye, Josie! *(Josie moves from locker, carrying plastic bags filled with her belongings, to Maureen. The women look at each other for a moment, silently, sadly. Suddenly, they hug.)*
JOSIE. I'll call you later, Reenie!
MAUREEN. *(Sadly.)* I'd better go. *(Turns; exits. Josie moves forward, carrying her belongings, ready to leave.)*
JOSIE. What a miserable "effin' " day, huh? Call me, Porker, huh?
PORKER. Uh, yuh, sure, Jose, sure ...
JOSIE. See ya', Flo ... *(Josie starts to exit; Florence stops her.)*
FLORENCE. Who's gonna' take Arlyne and Ruthie's stuff to them?
JOSIE. Want me to?
FLORENCE. Uh uh. It's okay. I'll take it. I just didn't want you stickin' me with the errand. Long as you offered no matter ... I'll take it to them ...
JOSIE. That reminds me. I left a whole bunch'a ice cream and

stuff in the freezer ... *(Josie exits into freezer. Florence looks at Porker.)*
FLORENCE. You and Josie are doin' it, huh?
PORKER. What's with you?
FLORENCE. *(Imitates Josie.) Call me, Porker, will ya?*
PORKER. Don't talk stupid ... *(Pauses.)* It's none of your business ... *(Smiles.)*
FLORENCE. I knew it! *(Josie exits refrigerator; crosses to Porker, winks at him, exits, carrying bag of ice cream containers.)*
JOSIE. See you guys ... How's about I call you after supper, Floey? About 6:30?
FLORENCE. 6:30's fine ... *(Josie, by habit, pulls her timecard from the rack and "punches out". The clock's bell rings, sharply. Florence and Porker turns around, startled. They smile. Josie shrugs, smiles, exits the play. There is a pause. Florence turns to Porker, who looks down.)* I s'pose with Jose you get more for your money ...
PORKER. I won't dignify that smart remark ...
FLORENCE. You wanna' go out with me, Porker?
PORKER. Tonight like?
FLORENCE. Tonight, tomorrow night ...
PORKER. You know I do.
FLORENCE. Okay. We'll go out.
PORKER. That is *great!*
FLORENCE. What's gonna' become of us, Porker?
PORKER. In what way?
FLORENCE. Life is so full of shit ... *(She looks about the room; sadly.)* My motha' was thirty years here ... breading, wrapping. For what, huh?
PORKER. Come onnn. She *loved* it!
FLORENCE. *(Smiles.)* She did, yuh ... *(Pauses.)* She's really lookin' awful, lately, Porker. Thirty years, not once bein' out sick, not once bein' late, not once leavin' at the bell, neither, and they lay her off like she did somethin' wrong. I mean, that's what she's thinkin'. That's what she's tryin' ta' figure out: what wrong thing did she do that she got punished for? She's got nothin' ... Nobody's got nothin' ... None of us: none of the old people ... I mean the real

people: the *Gloucester* people ... I'm gonna' end up just like my motha', Porker; wicked miserable lonely, cookin' too much food when somebody finally breaks down and visits, chewin' stuff over and over again that happened years and years ago, makin' out that it was good, makin' out that somethin' that happened to her mattered ... goin' over and over the past. No plans for nothin' ...
PORKER. Come onn, Floey. Sally'll hook up to something, soon. He's workin' on four five possibilities ... *(Shrugs; smiles.)* We can collect ... The weather's good ...
FLORENCE. I guess ... What're we s'pose ta' do now, Porker?
PORKER. Us? I dunno' ... we'll clean up. We'll put out the lights, we'll go home, wash ourselves up, you'll cook somethin' up for Bradley and Emily, I'll eat some of my sistah' Rose's horrendous cooking, we'll go ta' sleep, get up in the morning' and face the fact we got no jobs, kill the day, maybe meet up and go down ta' the Capri in Beverly, get sick on pizza, catch a movie, get married ... I dunno. Why don't you go home, start pickin' out somethin' to wear? *(There is a noise overhead. Porker and Florence are both startled; look up.)* What gives?
FLORENCE. Somebody's breakin' in! *(Two legs drop into sight: garbadine slacks, black wing-tip shoes ... we've seen this costume.)*
PORKER. Sal! *(Sally drops down, on to the top of the breading machine, eyes wild with determination.)*
SALLY. I've been up on the roof, watchin' and listenin' to what everybody's been sayin' about me. I know that you and my friend Martino here have always been attracted to each other and that now you're both available for each other and all, so, before you go runnin' off with my friend Martino here, I want to tell you something, Florence.
FLORENCE. What's this?
PORKER. *(To Florence.)* He's always been jealous of us ... ever since 2nd grade! *(To Sal.)* Nobody's runnin' off, Sal. We're just talkin'! Honest to Christ!
SALLY. Florence, I ... I love you, Florence.
PORKER. Your foot's in the breading, Sal. Watch it!

SALLY. I've got'ta talk to Florence, Alfred ... *alone*, okay?
PORKER. Yuh, well, I can see that. I'll wait in the freezer ... *(Porker starts off. Florence yells out.)*
FLORENCE. Stay, Porker! *(Porker starts to stay.)*
SALLY. I have to talk to her, Pork ...
PORKER. She wants me to stay, Sal ...
SALLY. Porker, please ... I'm askin' ya' like a friend ...
PORKER. I ... *(Exchanges a glance with Florence.)* I'll stay, but I won't listen. *(Porker gets mop. He starts to mop, as he did at start of play. He looks around at Sally.)* I'm not listening. Honest to God. *(Mops a moment; calls out.)* What? I'm not listening. *(Sally whispers to Florence, as confidentially as he can manage to be.)*
SALLY. I love you, Florence. I couldn't go off without you hearin' that from my mouth.
FLORENCE. What about your stitches?
SALLY. My stitches can wait, Flo. I'll risk it.
FLORENCE. Just be careful you don't fall off the breader.
SALLY. I'm leaving Carmella, Florence. I decided.
PORKER. What are you *sayin'*, Sal? *(Florence throws a stay-out-of-this look to Porker. Porker returns to his mopping.)*
FLORENCE. What are you sayin', Sal?
SALLY. Jesus, Florence, pay attention! All my life, you've been *it*. When we were in 4th grade, I was already serious: in love with you! Of all the girls I've ever loved, you've always been *it*, Florence. I was just now driving up to the hospital for stitches and I'm thinkin' to myself "Sally, you're screwing it up with Florence in a big way. You're gonna' get your stitches, you're gonna' go home to Carmella, and that will be it for the next forty fifty years until you get some devastating dread disease and croak!" I'm doin' it, Florence. Even though Carmella will probably drown herself off Bass Rocks and my kids will turn out to be junkies. Also, I'm a Catholic, so my soul will no-doubt-about-it burn in hell for forty fifty thousand years, but I'm doin' it ... for you, Flo. *(Sally stares into space, suddenly silent. Porker and Florence look at each other. He looks up at Florence, eyeball to eyeball. He makes his pronouncement.)* I'm moving in with you, Florence. I'm leaving Carmella and the Church. As soon as my

divorce comes through, you and I are getting married.
FLORENCE. Are you asking me to marry you, Sal?
SALLY. Isn't what I said clear?
FLORENCE. *(After a substantial pause.)* No.
SALLY. No, it's not clear, or, no, you won't marry me?
FLORENCE. No, I won't marry you. *(Porker laughs, discreetly, turning away from Sally as best he can.)* Go home to Carmella, Sal. It's okay. Go home.
SALLY. I don't want you to hate me, Florence.
FLORENCE. I don't hate you, Sal. But, that's no reason to be married to you.
SALLY. *(He means what he says.)* I'm sorry, Florence.
FLORENCE. Me, too ... *(Suddenly, the back door opens. To everyone's amazement, Marlena enters, looks around, sees Sal.)*
MARLENA. I'm *fryin'* out there! It must be a hundred! You said "Five minutes" about a half hour ago! I gotta' get home!
PORKER. Jesus, Sal ...
FLORENCE. Jesus, Sal ...
SALLY. I told her not to come in, no matter what! *(Yells at Marlena.)* Didn't I tell you not to come in, no matter what? *(To Florence.)* This doesn't mean there's anything between me and her at all, Florence. She's just drivin' me ...
PORKER. How come you need a ride? Where's your car?
SALLY. *Stay out of this!* *(To Florence.)* Can I call you later, Florence?
FLORENCE. I ... for what?
SALLY. For *talking!* To talk to you!
MARLENA. I'm not getting in the middle of *nothin'!* I'm goin'! *(Marlena leaves in a huff, slamming door behind her as she goes. Sally looks worried. He's in a bind. Florence sees this and laughs.)*
FLORENCE. You'd better go.
SALLY. I'd better.
FLORENCE. You'd better ...
SALLY. *(Wants to stay and wants to go. Makes moves in both directions. Suddenly, he points at Porker.)* This was all private stuff, Martino!

PORKER. Hey, c'mon, huh? Mum's the word, Sal. Trust me. *(Sal starts to speak again to Florence but has nothing further to say. He looks at her and then at Porker.)*
SALLY. We've only got each other, right? We came in together, we go out together. That's Friends. *(Sally exits the play. Florence stares after him a while, thoughtfully. She turns and sees that Porker has mopped and tidied the work-area: it sparkles.)*
FLORENCE. What's with you? The plant's closed ...
PORKER. No reason to leave it filthy ...
FLORENCE. You're okay, Porker ... *(She starts to weep; doesn't.)*
PORKER. Yuh, well ...
FLORENCE. *(Tries not to weep; turns; starts to exit.)* See you around, huh?
PORKER. *(Stops her; sings, with Sinatra voice.)* "Love was just a glance away ... a warm, romantic chance away ..." *(Florence stops, laughs; turns and faces Porker; sings.)*
FLORENCE. "If you want a dooo riiiight allll niiight's womannn ..."
PORKER. You wanna' get married, Florence?
FLORENCE. What's this?
PORKER. If you're carrying and all, you oughta' be married ...
FLORENCE. What about Carmella and their kids?
PORKER. To *me*, Florence. I mean to me. *(There is a long, long pause.)*
FLORENCE. I think your mind's snapped, Porker, 'counta' the plant closin' down and all ...
PORKER. A baby oughta' have a fatha' ... *(Florence stares at Porker, suddenly cries.)* You don't have to answer right away. We'll be goin' out and all ... *(Porker moves to Florence, wants to embrace her, thinks better of it.)* I'll ask you again, maybe Tuesday night, say ... *(Pauses. Florence is really in trouble: She is sobbing.)* Are you cryin' 'cause I asked you to marry me?
FLORENCE. That isn't it ...
PORKER. I can understand and all ... getting stuck, just 'cause of yo'r situation and all ...

FLORENCE. *(Looks around at empty plant.)* This is all I know how ta' do, Porker. Me, my mother, my grandmother, all of us ... We know the fish business. *(Pauses.)* I've got nothing left to teach my children, Porker. They're gonna look at me and that's what I'm gonna think ... *(She sobs, chokes back her tears, continues.)* I got nothin' left to teach my children ... *(Porker looks sadly at Florence; tries to cheer her.)*

PORKER. Don't cry, Flo, huh? *(Motions to boxes on assembly line.)* It's only *work* ... *(Shrugs.)* It ain't *life!* *(Florence sobs. Porker goes to her; they embrace. He sobs as well. Music in: repeat of lyric that started scene: Otis Redding, singing "She may be weary ... young girls do get weary ... wearing that same shaggy dress ... " The light begins to fade. Florence sobs in Porker's arms. They stand under one of the industrial lights over assembly line: in their own "natural" spotlight. The stage lights are now out.*

Otis Redding completes lyric: " ... try a little tenderness ... "

And the industrial light — their spotlight — fades to black.)

THE PLAY IS OVER.

Gloucester, Massachusetts - Dulwich (England) - New York, New York, October, 1985 - February 1989.

COSTUME PLOT
(Costume Design by Mimi Maxmen)

FLO
Shorts
Tank top
Stretch lace body suit
Sandals
Earrings
Gold chain
Purse
Watch
Faded jeans
Muscle shirt
Down vest
Work shoes — deck shoes
Hair net

ARLYNE
Yellow uniform top w/matching pants
Space shoes
Purse
Shoe bag
Wedding band
Cardigan
Half socks
Nurse's lace-up shoes
Hair net

RUTHIE
Pregnancy pad
Sun dress
T shirt

Wedge sandals
Wedding band w/small engagement ring
Earrings
Barrettes
Cross
Dr. Scholl's wooden sandals w/heavy sox
Canvas tote
Pale green uniform smock
Hair net
(Exits after baby's birth wearing:)
    Catherine Shimma's lab coat

MARLENA
Cut-off jeans
Leotard
Large socks
Tennis shoes
Wedding band
Earrings
Shoulder bag
Yellow uniform smock
Turquoise zip-front hooded sweat shirt
Hair net

JOSIE
Slacks
Blouse
Sandals
Wedding band
Earrings
Watch
Lacey bra
Large purse
Pink uniform pants
Pink, short-sleeve uniform top
Pale blue, printed work style shirt

Tennis shoes
Socks
Hair net

MAUREEN
Jeans
Sleeveless cotton top
Tennis shoes
Socks
Back pack
Barrettes
Wedding band
Earrings
Pale green zip-front hooded sweat shirt
Pink uniform smock
Hair net

CATHERINE
White uniform slacks
White, short-sleeved uniform blouse
Pumps
Earrings
Watch
Wedding band w/engagement ring
Hair combs
Shoulder bag/brief case
White lab coat
Nurse's shoes
Hair net

SAL
Black polyester gabardine slacks
Black belt
Pink shirt
Tie
Dark shoes

Socks
Wedding band
Watch
Lab coat

PORKER
Khaki work slacks
Khaki work shirt
Work boots
White socks
Singlet undershirts
Watch
Watch cap
Denim apron

ISRAEL HOROVITZ: CURRENT BIOGRAPHY

ISRAEL HOROVITZ was born in Wakefield, Massachusetts. His first play, "The Comeback", was written at age 17, and premiered at Emerson College, Boston. In the 30 years that have followed, some 50 Horovitz plays have been translated and performed in more than 20 languages, worldwide. Among the best-known Horovitz plays are: "The Indian Wants The Bronx", which introduced Al Pacino and John Cazale; "Line", which introduced Richard Dreyfuss (a revival of "Line" is now in its 14th year, off-Broadway); "It's Called The Sugar Plum", which introduced Marsha Mason and Jill Clayburgh; "Rats"; "Morning" of the Horovitz-McNally-Melfi tryptych "Morning Noon and Night"; "The Wakefield Plays", a seven-play cycle including "Hopscotch", "The 75th", "Alfred The Great", "Our Father's Failing", "Alfred Dies", "Stage Directions" and "Spared"; "Mackerel"; "The Primary English Class", which starred Diane Keaton in its NYC premiere; and "The Good Parts". For the past several years, Mr. Horovitz has been at work on a cycle of plays set in his adopted hometown, Gloucester, Massachusetts, all of which have had their world premieres at The Gloucester Stage Company, a theatre founded by Horovitz 10 years ago, and which he still serves as its Artistic Director/Producer. Among Horovitz's Gloucester Plays are: "The Widow's Blind Date"; "Park Your Car In Harvard Yard", which was workshopped at the Manhattan Theatre Club with Burgess Meredith and Ellen Burstyn; "Henry Lumper", which played to SRO audiences for several months at the Gloucester Stage Company, and re-opened, off-Broadway, in January, in a GSC/Working Theatre collaboration; "North Shore Fish", which was a success at the WPA Theatre, off-Broadway, and is slated for transfer to Broadway; last season's Hudson Guild Theatre entry, "Year Of The Duck"; "Firebird At Dogtown"; "Fighting Over Beverly", which was commissioned by England's Hampstead Theatre Company, where the play will have its premiere next season; and "Sunday Runners In The Rain", which was workshopped at the N.Y. Shakespeare Festival. Other recent

Horovitz plays include "The Former One-On-One Basketball Champion", which was produced last season in Seattle, starring former Boston Celtics great, Bill Russell; and Horovitz's "Sault Ste. Marie Trilogy": "Today, I Am A Fountain Pen"; "A Rosen By Any Other Name"; and "The Chopin Playoffs". His short comedy "Faith" was seen off-Broadway, earlier this season in the Horovitz-McNally-Melfi 20th reunion triptych "Faith, Hope and Charity". Horovitz has recently completed four original screenplays: "Deuce", which he is producing for Columbia Pictures; "Payofski's Discovery", for Warner Bros.; "Letters To Iris", for ITC Films; and "The Pan" for M-G-M. Other Horovitz screenplays include "The Strawberry Statement"; "Author! Author!"; and "A Man In Love" (written with Diane Kurys). Horovitz has won numerous awards, including the OBIE (twice), the Emmy, The French Critics' Prize, the NY Drama Desk Award, an Award in Literature of The American Academy of Arts and Letters, The Eliot Norton Prize, and many others. He is married to the former Gillian Adams, the British marathoner, and is the father of five children, Rachael, Matthew, Adam, Hannah and Oliver Horovitz. The Horovitz family divides its time among homes in Gloucester, Massachusetts, NYC's Greenwich Village, and London's Dulwich Village.

(June, 1989.)

ESCAPE ⓪

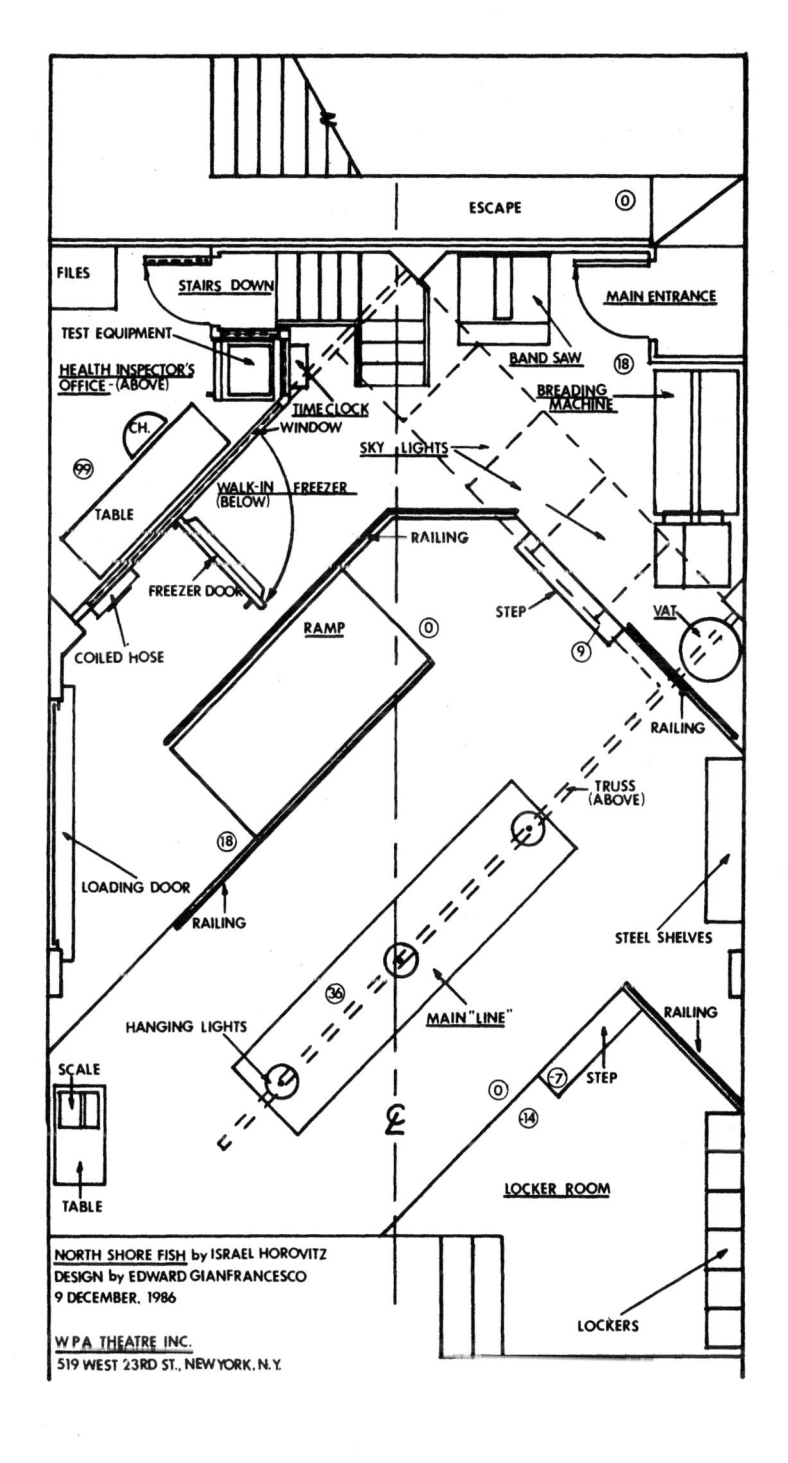

FILES

STAIRS DOWN

MAIN ENTRANCE

TEST EQUIPMENT

HEALTH INSPECTOR'S
OFFICE - (ABOVE)

BAND SAW ⑱

TIME CLOCK

WINDOW

BREADING MACHINE

CH.

⑨⑨

SKY LIGHTS

TABLE

WALK-IN FREEZER
(BELOW)

RAILING

FREEZER DOOR

STEP

VAT

RAMP ⓪

COILED HOSE

RAILING

⑨

LOADING DOOR

⑱

RAILING

TRUSS (ABOVE)

STEEL SHELVES

㊱

HANGING LIGHTS

MAIN "LINE"

RAILING

SCALE

⓪ ⑦ STEP

⑭

LOCKER ROOM

TABLE

LOCKERS

NORTH SHORE FISH by ISRAEL HOROVITZ
DESIGN by EDWARD GIANFRANCESCO
9 DECEMBER, 1986

WPA THEATRE INC.
519 WEST 23RD ST., NEW YORK, N.Y.

www.audible.com